P9-EFJ-991

What People Are Saying About Apostle Guillermo Maldonado and *Breakthrough Prayer*...

If you think of prayer as a duty—think again! Apostle Maldonado reminds us that prayer is, first and foremost, a place in the Spirit where we are united with our heavenly Father and are empowered for His purposes. It is where we experience the glory of His presence to shatter strongholds and set captives free. Learn to enter God's presence through *breakthrough prayer*, creating a spiritual atmosphere in which He moves mightily to heal, deliver, and transform lives. This is prayer that God always hears—and answers!

—*Paula White*
Senior Pastor, New Destiny Christian Center, Apopka, FL
Host, *Paula White Today*

Many do not pray because they don't see results. If you only knew that nothing happens on earth without prayer. Apostle Maldonado's teaching will not only show you how to have breakthrough after breakthrough in prayer, but prayer will become your greatest joy!

—*Sid Roth*
Host, *It's Supernatural!*

Breakthrough Prayer is one of the most revelatory books I know of on the subject of intercessory prayer. If you are frustrated that you are not seeing answers to your prayers, this book is for you. If you want to see quicker answers, this book is also for you!

—*Dr. Cindy Jacobs*
Generals International

Apostle Guillermo Maldonado is leading an incredibly powerful movement of God across the globe. I've had the honor of witnessing his love of and devotion to the presence of God, which cultivate an atmosphere for the Lord to move in signs, wonders, and miracles. His ministry has touched countless lives with the redemptive power of Jesus!

His new book, *Breakthrough Prayer*, is written with a spirit of excellence, a mark of everything Maldonado puts his hands to. This book is a representation of his drive and passion for the bride of Christ to be prepared for and partner with what Jesus wants to do on the earth. In its pages, you will not find empty words to recite to God, but rather divine insight and activation into two-way communication with the Father.

—*Kris Vallotton*
Senior Associate Leader, Bethel Church, Redding, CA
Cofounder, Bethel School of Supernatural Ministry
Author of thirteen books, including *The Supernatural Ways of Royalty, Heavy Rain*, and *Poverty, Riches and Wealth*

Breakthrough Prayer is an outstanding book on the preciousness and power of prayer. In this wonderful new book, you will be instructed in how to build a personal relationship with Father God. Without question, you will gain much-needed insights into the priority of sincere prayer, and you will be taught how to enter into the secret place of prayer. Your life will be enriched as you study the profound insights from this book, and you will learn how to grow in prayer, moving into a higher spiritual realm. God moves when we pray! Remember, through prayer, we are forging the future and shaping the now. Don't waste any time—get this book and start your spiritual journey towards a deeper, more committed prayer life.

—*Bobby Conner*
Eagles View Ministries

I love Pastor Guillermo's teachings on prayer because I have personally witnessed him praying. Prayer opens doors to the supernatural, and I am eager to meditate on his book. Every believer needs this teaching in order to mature as a Christian. I have learned much from Pastor Guillermo and his wife, Ana, on this vital topic, and I am expecting more breakthroughs on prayer.

—*Marilyn Hickey*
Marilyn Hickey Ministries

Apostle Maldonado is an anointed vessel of God. His message is from the Holy Spirit, and Apostle is full of insight and revelation. He is gifted at bringing out hidden truths. Your spiritual walk with the Lord will be greatly enhanced after reading this book.

—*Dr. Don Colbert, MD*
New York Times best-selling author

BREAK THROUGH PRAYER

WHERE GOD ALWAYS HEARS AND ANSWERS

GUILLERMO MALDONADO

WHITAKER
HOUSE

Note: This book is not intended to provide medical advice or to take the place of medical advice and treatment from your personal physician. Neither the publisher nor the author nor the author's ministry takes any responsibility for any possible consequences from any action taken by any person reading or following the information in this book. If readers are taking prescription medications, they should consult with their physicians and not take themselves off prescribed medicines without the proper supervision of a physician. Always consult your physician or other qualified health care professional before undertaking any change in your physical regimen, whether fasting, diet, medications, or exercise.

Unless otherwise indicated, all Scripture quotations are taken from the *New King James Version*, © 1979, 1980, 1982, 1984 by Thomas Nelson, Inc. Used by permission. Scripture quotations marked (KJV) are taken from the King James Version of the Holy Bible. Scripture quotations marked (ASV) are taken from the American Standard Edition of the Revised Version of the Holy Bible. Scripture quotations marked (NIV) are taken from the *Holy Bible, New International Version*®, NIV®, © 1973, 1978, 1984, 2011 by Biblica, Inc.® Used by permission of Zondervan. All rights reserved worldwide. www.zondervan.com. The "NIV" and "New International Version" are trademarks registered in the United States Patent and Trademark Office by Biblica, Inc.®

Boldface type in the Scripture quotations indicates the author's emphasis. The forms LORD and GOD (in small caps) in Bible quotations represent the Hebrew name for God *Yahweh* (Jehovah), while *Lord* and *God* normally represent the name *Adonai*, in accordance with the Bible version used.

Definitions of Hebrew and Greek words are taken from the electronic version of *Strong's Exhaustive Concordance of the Bible*, STRONG (© 1980, 1986, and assigned to World Bible Publishers, Inc. Used by permission. All rights reserved.), or *Nueva Concordancia Strong Exhaustiva*, © 2002 by Editorial Caribe, Inc., Nashville, TN.

Dictionary definitions are taken from *Merriam-Webster.com*, 2018, http://www.merriam-webster.com.

KJM Editors: Jose M. Anhuaman and Gloria Zura
Cover Design: Juan Salgado

BREAKTHROUGH PRAYER:
Where God Always Hears and Answers

Guillermo Maldonado
14100 SW 144th Ave. ♦ Miami, FL 33186
King Jesus Ministry / ERJ Publicaciones
www.kingjesus.org / www.ERJPub.org

ISBN: 978-1-64123-161-9 ♦ eBook ISBN: 978-1-64123-167-1
Printed in the United States of America
© 2018 by Guillermo Maldonado

Whitaker House
1030 Hunt Valley Circle ♦ New Kensington, PA 15068
www.whitakerhouse.com

Library of Congress Cataloging-in-Publication Data:
LC record available at https://lccn.loc.gov/2018033856

No part of this book may be reproduced or transmitted in any form or by any means, electronic or mechanical—including photocopying, recording, or by any information storage and retrieval system—without permission in writing from the publisher. Please direct your inquiries to permissionseditor@whitakerhouse.com.

1 2 3 4 5 6 7 8 9 10 11 ᴂ 25 24 23 22 21 20 19 18

CONTENTS

FOREWORD

I believe in the most powerful tool Christians have: prayer. Many years ago, I was on the verge of either the greatest breakthrough I'd ever had or the largest breakdown in my life. We had just planted our church in Los Angeles during the Great Recession of 2007. L.A. was hit by strikes, and many of them were in the labor fields of the entertainment industry. The majority of our budding church was made up of entertainers. We were believing for so much, but it wasn't until we began to practice many of the principles covered in this very book that we had a true tipping point. While the majority of the city (and even many other churches) was suffering, we began to build and thrive in our community. It went totally against the grain, and we completely owed it to the power of encountering the Holy Spirit through *a deliberate lifestyle of prayer.*

Time and time again, I have pressed into prayer as if my life depended on it, and you know what? It has! And your life depends on it, too, as well as the well-being of your family, your industry, your nation, and your world. The church is sitting on the power to shift nations, atmospheres, people groups, and justice issues, and all we have to do is pray. We can look into the heart of the Father and bring agreement here on earth, in our spheres of influence.

Ephesians 1:17 is so key to fullness. In it, Paul prayed over the Ephesians to have the spirit of wisdom and revelation so they could really know Jesus the way He wants to be known. The heart of Jesus is the most beautiful of any you will ever know. Many people enter into the saving grace of Jesus without ever knowing the full benefit of what can happen if they go deeper into His fullness—because it takes a very intentional walk through prayer. Prayer is either a relational device or a chore, depending on how you approach it and what your personal motivation is within the pursuit.

In John 17, we get a very personal glimpse into Jesus's prayer life when He was intimately pouring His heart out to the Father. We see how deeply He loved us because of how He was including us and asking for the Father to give us the same divine union He experienced. His primary desire was, and is, for us to have this place of really connected relationship with the Father that brings a manifest result.

Modern Christianity has minimized the powerful prayer lifestyle that the early church used as its lifeline. I love Apostle Maldonado's book because it calls for a return to the value of prayer. It gives understanding into the modern ways in which God is working, demonstrates how to apply our most powerful weapon in our arsenal (as Christians), and builds our incentives for prayer. His experience and the collective perspective he includes give a new foundation for the power of true prayer, one that will build you up. Power-producing, thought-provoking, solution-bringing, intimacy-building—these are all the things that happen when engaging in prayer through the model that Apostle Maldonado has set forth in this exciting new book!

—*Shawn Bolz*
www.bolzministries.com
Author, *Translating God, God Secrets,*
and *Keys to Heaven's Economy*
Host, *Exploring the Prophetic* Podcast

PREFACE

Breakthrough Prayer is an urgent call to the body of Christ because of the times in which we live. Many books on prayer have been written over the centuries—a number of them in just the last few years. This is as it should be, because developing a practice of prayer has always been an essential part of our relationship with our heavenly Father and the means of our spiritual growth.

But now, more than ever, the body of Christ and individual believers need to *press in to prayer*—increasing the intensity of our devotion to the Lord as our *"first love"* (Revelation 2:4) and raising the level of our intercession to meet the growing spiritual challenges and opposition we face. This can only occur as we understand and begin to practice *breakthrough* prayer that takes us beyond apathy, fear, the limitations of the natural world, and demonic hindrances to become the victorious church God has called us to be. It can only happen as we move beyond the natural realm and into the supernatural realm of heavenly power.

In chapter 8, "Keys to Breakthrough Prayer," I write:

Breakthrough prayer generates an abrupt, violent, and sudden rupture of what is hindering us, pushing us beyond that limitation and into freedom. Breakthrough prayer must be engaged in persistently and consistently until we sense that something has broken in the spiritual realm, and until what we are asking for manifests. With a breakthrough, what we need is brought from the spiritual world to the natural world, so that we can see it in a visible or tangible demonstration of God's power or provision.

Today, the people of God need breakthroughs in all areas of life—in their personal life, family, business, education, health, emotions, and more. This world needs breakthroughs by the power of the gospel for salvation, healing, and deliverance. The church needs breakthroughs to become the true bride of Christ and fulfill its purpose on earth.

My prayer is that this book will ignite in you a passion for prayer and that the Lord will use it to further these purposes:

Restoration. I have traveled in over sixty countries, and in most of these nations, even among Christians, only a small percentage of the people regularly pray. We must develop an appetite for and a commitment to the priority of prayer—as important to our spiritual lives as oxygen is to our bodies. We can be restored to a close relationship with God as we learn to live continually in His presence.

Reception. We are in a season of spiritual harvest in which all the prayers that believers have offered—from the prayers of the patriarchs to ours today—whose answers have not yet been revealed on earth will now be manifested. The "bowl" of the saints' prayers mentioned in the book of Revelation is already filled and ready to be poured out on the earth. We must be prepared to appropriate and receive these answers!

Preparation. All the signs point to the nearness of the second coming of Christ. Only prayer can prepare our hearts for this momentous event of receiving our King, and empower us to endure the spiritual, emotional, and physical pressures leading up to that time.

Perseverance. The atmosphere on the earth has become spiritually dark. We are in a period of increased opposition from the enemy as we draw closer to the day of Christ's return. Overcoming this kind of darkness necessitates a higher level of spiritual power and authority. Jesus taught us to "watch *and* pray." We must learn to do so now!

Let us commit to prayer—to *breakthrough prayer*—that can enable us to live in victory now and lead us to the celebration of our coming King!

> *I pray that the eyes of your heart may be enlightened in order that you may know the hope to which he has called you, the riches of his glorious inheritance in his holy people, and his incomparably great power for us who believe.* (Ephesians 1:18–19 NIV)

1

THE SECRET PLACE OF PRAYER

*"But you, when you pray, go into your room, and when you have
shut your door, pray to your Father who is in the secret place;
and your Father who sees in secret will reward you openly."*
—Matthew 6:6

Prayer is a *place*. A secret place in the Spirit. There, our relationship with God is established; and from there, everything we ask according to His will is given to us. When Jesus was on earth, He would often pray alone in the desert, but we can choose any place and dedicate it specifically for prayer. In the natural, we all need a physical place to represent the spiritual place where we meet daily with God. However, in order to fully experience the presence of God, we must recognize that the atmosphere of that place is more important than the place itself. There is nowhere on earth (or in the universe) where the presence of God is absent, no matter how hidden it may be. Nevertheless, although the Lord is everywhere, He does not *manifest* His presence everywhere. His presence manifests only where He is worshipped *"in spirit and truth"* (John 4:23–24).

Jesus taught that when we pray, we should go into our *"room"* (place of prayer), shut ourselves in with God, and speak to Him with faith and trust, as a little child speaks to their father. Our heavenly Father will always be waiting for us there. When we have learned to pray in the secret place, we will find that nothing and no one else is more important to us than God. In that place, we are alone with our Creator—the King of Kings, the Almighty, the One who knows everything, including the state of each person's heart. (See, for example, 1 John 3:20; Acts 1:24.) There, we are submerged in such sweet communion with the Lord that we don't want to leave that place; we are passionate about being alone with our heavenly Father, and that pleases Him. Being in the presence of God is so wonderful that we no longer worry about other people or about our problems, fears, and doubts; not even the thought of gaining riches or fame interests us. If, while we are praying, we are thinking about other things, we are not truly in God's presence because there He becomes our complete reality.

What is the secret place of prayer like?

The Secret Place Is...

1. The Place Where God's Presence Is Revealed and Manifested

> *Therefore, brethren, having boldness to enter the Holiest by the blood of Jesus, by a new and living way which He consecrated for us, through the veil, that is, His flesh, and having a High Priest over the house of God, let us draw near with a true heart in full assurance of faith....* (Hebrews 10:19–22)

Jesus's sacrifice on the cross gives us access to the presence of God, and prayer is the place where that access occurs. We cannot pray without first recognizing we are in God's presence. In fact, we don't pray for the purpose of entering into His presence; we pray *because* we are in His presence. To pray is to recognize we have a divine appointment where we can speak face-to-face with a holy God. Because we cannot talk with an absent God, it is necessary for us to know that He is present and He hears and responds to us. The Scripture says that when King Solomon finished building the temple, the Lord appeared to Him and said, *"I have heard your prayer and your supplication that you have made before Me"* (1 Kings 9:3).

> Every prayer begins when we recognize
> we are in the presence of God.

Remember, no matter where we go, God is with us. Even if we don't feel His presence, He is there. The psalmist says, *"If I ascend into heaven, You are there; if I make my bed in hell, behold, You are there"* (Psalm 139:8). Through the fire and the storm, in tribulations and persecutions, through loneliness and fear, He is always with us, because He has promised to be there. Jesus gave us His word that He would be with us *"even unto the end of the world"* (Matthew 28:20 KJV).

True prayer, therefore, includes a consciousness of being in the presence of God Almighty. To be in God's presence, you need to set all your affection on Him; this means fixing your attention and thoughts on Him, focusing completely on His person. When we do this, eternity is pulled into the realm of time.

So He [Jesus] Himself often withdrew into the wilderness and prayed. Now it happened on a certain day, as He was teaching, that there were Pharisees and teachers of the law sitting by, who *had come out of every town of Galilee, Judea, and Jerusalem. **And the power of the Lord was present to heal them.***

(Luke 5:16–17)

Every day, Jesus made sure He was in communication with the Father and filled with His presence. This is why, after He would return from the place of prayer, He would radiate power. When the multitudes approached Him seeking healing and deliverance, Jesus only had to declare the word, and supernatural breakthrough occurred. After spending time in the presence of God, Jesus didn't need to pray for people, because the atmosphere He carried—which He had built with His Father—produced instant miracles, signs, and wonders. The Father saw Jesus's prayers in the secret place and rewarded Him publicly.

> The proof that we are praying in the presence of God is that we become carriers of His presence.

I have had similar experiences after spending time in the secret place of prayer. I frequently see supernatural manifestations happen around me. For example, I have seen people be healed without my touching them or praying for them. Paralytics get up from their wheelchairs, demonic spirits manifest in public places, and people weep for no apparent reason. These things happen because the atmosphere of the presence of God shakes the kingdom of darkness—which, when confronted, cannot continue operating.

> Our consistency in prayer can be measured by the level of the presence and power of God that we carry.

The presence of God dwells within every believer at all times; it is not shut away somewhere in a church building. When we are fully aware of this reality and spend time in fellowship with our Father in the secret place, then wherever we go, we will carry the atmosphere of His presence; we will radiate His life, liberty, power, and glory. Anyone who moves in miracles, signs, and wonders understands this dynamic.

What atmosphere do you carry? What happens when you pray? As believers, we need to be filled with the atmosphere of heaven before we approach other people to pray for them. If you are a pastor or a leader in your church, don't wait for anyone else to build the atmosphere of God's presence during a service. You are called to bring the atmosphere of God there! As you do, people will perceive that you are different from others, because a man or woman who continually walks in the presence of God inevitably draws attention—to God's glory!

2. The Place Where We Come to Know God

Because God's presence is manifested to us in the secret place of prayer, it is there where we come to know the Father. *"This is eternal life, that they may know You, the only true God, and Jesus Christ whom You have sent"* (John 17:3). As we pray, God reveals Himself to us, and we are attracted to Him in an ever greater way. He places us under His care as His special treasure and as part of His very heart.

God wants us to see Him as He is; He longs to establish an intimate relationship with us, and for us to become one with Him as He is one with His Son Jesus. Jesus is one with the Father by nature, and through Him, we are children of God by adoption. (See, for example, John 10:30; Ephesians 1:4–6.) And prayer is the place where we can see God as He really is and receive His life.

3. The Place Where We Appropriate the Power of God

And when they had prayed, the place where they were assembled together was shaken; and they were all filled with the Holy Spirit, and they spoke the word of God with boldness.... And with great power the apostles gave witness to the resurrection of the Lord Jesus. And great grace was upon them all. (Acts 4:31, 33)

In the book of Acts, every time Christians got together to pray, the power of God manifested. This indicates to us that the church should never lack power. The enemy attacks the prayer life of churches and individual believers because he doesn't want them to have access to God's supernatural power and grace.

> Every time you pray, you have access to the power of God.

Prayer generates power. When someone prays in the secret place, they are empowered in the presence of God so they can go and pour out that power upon other people for healing, deliverance, and miracles. Remember, the Word says, "*Your Father who sees in secret will reward you openly.*" Power is our inheritance as children of God, but we can only use it legally, in a spiritual sense, through prayer that is part of an intimate relationship with the Father.

In Acts 2, we see that the disciples remained in prayer for several days, after which they were baptized in the Holy Spirit. Then Peter went out and proclaimed the message of the gospel; when he had preached for only a short while, three thousand souls were won for the kingdom of heaven. Many preachers today do the opposite—they pray for a few minutes and then preach for two hours; that is why they don't see people being saved and healed. The worst part is that they feel satisfied in doing this, while God's Word shows us that true prayer is confirmed by His power being tangibly and visibly demonstrated.

> Before giving us power, God wants us to have a relationship with Him.

4. The Place Where We Participate in Spiritual Activity

The Spirit of God is continually active on the earth. When you pray, you become a participant in what He is currently creating and doing in the world, and you begin to build spiritual environments in which He can work. Then, when you come into contact with other people, you impart some of that spiritual activity to them—in healings, miracles, anointing, and other manifestations.

> Prayer causes strong spiritual activity within us.

Sadly, much of the church today doesn't know how to pray; consequently, spiritual darkness has become thick on the earth. This generation lacks the spiritual depth that a life of prayer produces. Those who are preachers need to pray at the same level that they want their preaching to attain. In other words, the depth of our prayer life will determine the depth of our message. I give great importance to my time of prayer. The time I use to preach will never be more important than my time in prayer because I know that prayer generates the spiritual activity I am to release. I can't preach based only on my acquired knowledge of the Bible. To produce a supernatural movement, I must carry the activity of the Spirit with me as I speak.

> When a person's spirit is empty, they produce empty words. When a person's spirit is burning with the Holy Spirit, they release God's power through anointed words and generate spiritual activity.

5. The Place Where We Obtain Spiritual Authority

Spiritual authority belongs to all children of God by inheritance through Jesus. (See, for example, Luke 10:19.) However, as is the case with spiritual power, our use of spiritual authority is legal only while we maintain a relationship with our heavenly Father. And a significant way in which God imparts His authority to us is through prayer. For this reason, whenever our prayer life begins to diminish—in our individual lives or as the corporate church—our spiritual authority is weakened. Not only do we start to lose authority, but we also begin to lose the spiritual territories we have won from the enemy. Today, we live in extreme times in which the enemy is doing everything he can to diminish the power of the church. Therefore, every day, we need a greater level of spiritual authority, and for this we must *"pray without ceasing"* (1 Thessalonians 5:17).

We must recognize that the authority to deal with the enemy is given to us only while we are on earth. Beyond that, it is illegal to exercise it. Note that when it came time for Aaron, the brother of Moses, to die, his authority as high priest was removed from him and given to someone else when his garments were placed on his son Eleazar. *"Moses stripped Aaron of his garments and put them on Eleazar his son; and Aaron died there on the top of the mountain"* (Numbers 20:28). This means you cannot wait until you go to heaven to exercise the authority over Satan that Jesus has given you—you need to exercise it here and now. A believer without authority on earth will be an easy prey for Satan. Without a doubt, the enemy will come and oppress them; he may even destroy them. I have seen some men die as soon as they have lost their spiritual authority; others have suffered from spiritual drought. We must maintain a healthy fear, or reverence, of God, and walk in the authority He has given us.

Let me point out here that prayer consists of talking and communing with God; it is not the same as doing spiritual warfare against the enemy. Some believers try to do spiritual warfare against demons without operating under the proper spiritual authority to cast them out. Expelling demons is not about shouting at them or fighting with them, but about knowing and operating in our spiritual authority. There are evil spirits of high rank that require greater authority to be cast out than those of lower rank, and that authority is obtained through fasting and prayer. Jesus taught this truth to His disciples when, despite their many efforts, they couldn't cast out a demon that was tormenting a young man. The Lord said to them, *"This kind does not go out except by prayer and fasting"* (Matthew 17:21). Jesus had authority to cast out demons of all ranks, because He was a Man of continuous prayer who lived in complete obedience under His Father's authority.

> Prayer is the place where we obtain power in greater levels to deal with demons of greater rank.

6. The Place Where We Submit to the Lordship of Christ

Additionally, the secret place of prayer is where we surrender our will to God so the Lord can accomplish His will in us. It is also where the greater spiritual struggles take place for believers, because it's easier to say, "Jesus is my Provider" than it is to say, "Jesus is my Lord and the Owner of my life."

While He was on earth, Jesus submitted to the lordship of the Father. For example, when He knew it was time for Him to suffer death on the cross, He prayed, *"Father, if it is Your will, take this cup away from Me; nevertheless not My will, but Yours, be done"* (Luke 22:42). Furthermore, to become the Lord of all, Jesus had to fully submit to His Father's will. Today, if we want to operate in heavenly authority, we, too, need to be people of prayer who live in complete obedience to the Father. And every day, we must surrender our will to the lordship of Jesus Christ, because total submission is not something that is accomplished instantly; it is a surrender that happens progressively.

> Spiritual power and authority are obtained by submission to the lordship of Christ.

7. The Place of the Sufferings of Christ

That I may know Him and the power of His resurrection, and the fellowship of His sufferings, being conformed to His death.
(Philippians 3:10)

The apostle Peter wrote, *"Therefore, since Christ suffered for us in the flesh, arm yourselves also with the same mind, for he who has suffered in the flesh has ceased from sin"* (1 Peter 4:1). Prayer is the place of fellowship with the sufferings of Christ because it requires obedience and self-denial. Jesus told His disciples, *"Watch and pray, lest you enter into temptation. The spirit indeed is willing, but the flesh is weak"* (Mark 14:38). Our flesh is weak; therefore, most of the time, it doesn't want to pray. Yet if we want to see people's lives transformed for Christ, we have to voluntarily submit our spirits to God and pray, regardless of what we "feel" like doing.

It was after Christ had suffered on the cross physically, emotionally, and spiritually that God released His resurrection power and raised Him from the dead. God has to work *in* us before He can work *through* us and make us good stewards of His grace. If, as we pray, we allow God to show us the sin that has become rooted in our lives, and to lead us to repentance and forgiveness so that our sin is taken away, then we will know Christ and we will resemble Him in His suffering. Jesus was without sin, yet He took our sin on the cross. He endured all suffering to please the Father, to be united with His purposes, and to do His will on earth. The question is, are we willing to do the same?

8. The Place Where the Keys of the Kingdom Are Activated

And I will give you the keys of the kingdom of heaven, and whatever you bind on earth will be bound in heaven, and whatever you loose on earth will be loosed in heaven.   (Matthew 16:19)

The Hebrew words translated *"bind"* and *"loose"* were legal terms commonly used by rabbis, who interpreted the law and declared what was prohibited ("bound") and what was permitted ("loosed").[1] Jesus used the Hebrew expression of "binding and loosing" to communicate to Peter—and all believers—that He gives us spiritual authority on earth. That is why, when we pray, we declare and decree; in other words, we pass "laws" or "regulations" concerning what is allowed and not allowed according to the will of God because we have the authority to do it. And that authority is ratified in heaven because it originates in Christ and is part of His work on earth. (See, for example,

---

1. See, for example, http://www.jewishencyclopedia.com/articles/3307-binding-and-loosing, and http://www.truthortradition.com/articles/binding-and-loosing.

Matthew 16:17–19; Luke 4:18.) Thus, we can say that we declare to be legal on earth what is legal in heaven, and we declare to be illegal on earth what is illegal in heaven. Christ will ratify in heaven what we do on earth, in His name and in accordance with His Word.

For this reason—and because *"death and life are in the power of the tongue"* (Proverbs 18:21)—it is important for us to be aware of what we are praying. If someone speaks a declaration of poverty, they will see poverty, because their words have the power to create, even though that declaration is not spiritually legal. Likewise, if they confess sickness, they will likely bring sickness upon themselves or someone else, putting into effect a negative "law" in their life. In contrast, if they declare prosperity or health, that is what they will receive, and their declaration is legal because it is aligned with God's will. I exhort you today to change your negative confessions to come into agreement with heaven by declaring in prayer what the Spirit of God and His Word reveal to us. Then, you will have access to all the blessings and provision the kingdom has in store for you as a child of God.

9. The Place Where We Expand Our Territory

The secret place of prayer is also where we expand the capacity of our spirit and the size of our territory. Your prayer life will determine your spiritual "metron," that is, your measure or level of influence and government in the Spirit. Paul understood about spiritual spheres of influence, saying, *"We, however, will not boast beyond measure, but within the limits of the sphere which God appointed us—a sphere which especially includes you"* (2 Corinthians 10:13). As your prayer life grows, your territories (domains of ministry and influence) will expand; but as your territories expand, your prayer life must also increase. It is not enough to gain a territory; it is important to maintain it. That is why we can never stop praying.

> When a church's prayer life is constant,
> its territories will continually expand.
> When its prayer life is weak, it will end up
> losing what it had previously gained.

Again, when we stop praying, we begin to lose the authority we previously had. We also lose those things over which we no longer exercise authority. This means we relinquish spiritual territory rather than gain it. Have you lost things that you know you were supposed to have—for example, your health, marriage, children, house or other property, business, job, position, anointing, even your faith?

> We don't lose other things until we lose our territory.

Forty years ago, it was common to see people healed of cancer in church crusades because the church's prayers were full of strength and power. Christians had gained that territory in the Spirit. Today, however, it seems more and more believers die of cancer and other sicknesses, as well as lose their marriages, their children, and their homes, because the church has stopped praying. Little by little, it has lost the territories it had gained. Additionally, because the church as a whole has moved away from prayer over the last few decades, more believers have started to depend on the prayers of others rather than maintaining a strong prayer life themselves. Today, I encourage you to go into your prayer room, shut yourself in with God, and persevere until you recover everything that the enemy has stolen from you!

You cannot be complacent about prayer—you must pray until you obtain a breakthrough. Jesus used to pray all night, and by dawn, He had won territories that had been controlled by the enemy. His prayer was not casual; He was committed to dwelling in the presence of the Father, and this commitment yielded supernatural results. Additionally, in the book of Acts, we see that each time Jesus's disciples prayed, the Spirit of God descended powerfully, and lives were transformed. Likewise, we need to pray in such a way that God's Spirit moves, bringing great change.

I declare that you now enter a season in which you recover everything you have lost—health, possessions, houses, anointing, faith—everything comes back to you, in Jesus's name. But you must be aggressive in the Spirit! Recover it all, now, in the name of Jesus!

Every war starts with a desire to win resources and territories; in a spiritual sense, resources and territories can be gained or regained only through prayer.

10. The Place Where We Obtain the Favor of God

For You, O LORD, will bless the righteous; with favor You will surround him as with a shield. (Psalm 5:12)

God's favor in our lives is seen in the manifestation of His power that allows us access to things we otherwise would not have. The favor of God makes us irresistible to blessings, protection, prosperity—and much more. Unlike other spiritual bestowments, God's favor cannot be imparted from one believer to another. I cannot pray for someone else to receive the favor of God. Rather, God's favor is something that individual believers and churches attract. It comes as a result of their communion and close relationship with their heavenly Father. That is why, when a believer leaves that communion, they automatically lose the favor of God.

Enter the Secret Place

Everything I have described to this point is revelation about the secret place of prayer, where man meets his Creator and is transformed. God expects us to daily enter His presence—the place where spiritual power and activity are released—to know His heart and to receive His authority. He longs for us to enter the place of submission and suffering, where the keys of the kingdom are found, where we gain territories, and where we receive His favor.

The church of Jesus Christ needs to go back to that secret place, so that the Father who sees in secret will reward the church in public. And what is that reward? An eternal, close relationship with the Lord that makes us continual carriers of His supernatural presence. Let us enter that secret place! I assure you that when we do, we will be ready to be God's faithful remnant—the bride of Christ who ministers in His name to the world and awaits His second coming. Let us embrace the life of God and become one with the Father, His Son Jesus Christ, and the Holy Spirit. Outside of that, nothing else matters!

Activation

Dear reader, if you recognize that your prayer life is not what it should be, if you know you have been praying in merely a "religious" way, without being conscious of the presence of God, without power or spiritual activity in your daily life, I invite you to say the following prayer out loud:

Beloved God, I thank You for bringing this revelation of the secret place of prayer to me. I ask for forgiveness if, due to ignorance or a lack of passion, I have not known how to seek a relationship with You that leads me to be in Your presence. Today, I commit to walk in communion with You. I am conscious of being in Your presence, and I know that You are my greater Reality, my absolute Reality. When I'm in Your presence, nothing else matters! I access Your presence and become its carrier. I declare that in Your presence, I receive power, and that miracles are manifested among Your people. I declare that I participate in Your spiritual activity on earth, creating heavenly atmospheres for Your presence to come and minister to others, and I receive spiritual authority to destroy the works of the devil.

I remain in submission to the lordship of Christ, just as Jesus walked in submission to the Father while He was on earth. I participate in Christ's sufferings in order to manifest the power of His resurrection. I declare that my prayers activate the keys of the kingdom, to legally bind and loose the will of God on earth. I also declare that, as I keep growing in prayer, my territories and domains will expand. I proclaim that I am fully conscious of God's presence, of His fellowship, and of the power and authority our relationship releases. I pray this in the mighty name of Jesus, in the now. Amen!

Testimonies of Breakthrough Prayer

God Heals in the Middle of Praise

A few years ago, Belen, who comes from Spain, joined King Jesus church in Miami, along with her family. She is a pastor and one of the praise and worship leaders in our ministry. This is her testimony of breakthrough prayer:

Apostle Maldonado was preaching a series on "End-time Faith." I had been praying and asking God to increase my measure of faith to be aligned with the father of this church, and to be able to minister to the people and build their faith. One Sunday morning, God spoke to me and said, "Belen, I already gave you a new measure of faith." I answered Him, "Lord, I want to see Your healing power in the midst of praise. Do it from the start!" I came out empowered and full of faith to sing to God.

Right when we started praising, I heard the Lord tell me, "I will heal the people according to their faith." I started feeling that there were people with pain in their bones. Led by God, I told them to start dancing as an act of faith, regardless of the pain, and God healed several of them. Lastly, God spoke to me about a woman who had a heart condition. I called her to the altar for the purpose of praising God in faith. I bound and rebuked the spirit of death, and I declared the life of God upon her. Some days later, she came to the altar to testify that, soon after that service, she went to get some new medical tests. Her doctor was amazed to confirm that her heart was completely healed. The glory be to God for all He did that day!

A Creative Miracle in the Brain

Armando and Aracely are a couple from Arizona, United States. Aracely was facing an extreme health situation, but thanks to my relationship with God and prayer, the Holy Spirit guided me to release a powerful miracle in her life. The following is Armando's account of what happened:

> During a time of ministry at CAP [the yearly Apostolic and Prophetic Conference hosted by King Jesus Ministry], Apostle Maldonado said God had revealed to him in prayer that He would restore organs and create bones where they were missing. At that time, my wife had been suffering a terrible headache for nine days. At the hospital, they had detected bleeding in her brain that they couldn't explain. They had to do emergency surgery because, according to the doctors, her brain had moved seven millimeters to one side, and that was a deadly condition. The doctors didn't want to talk to me because I always declared she was healed. I knew God would do a miracle at CAP.
>
> My wife went to CAP feeling very sick, with a severe headache and hypersensitivity to light and noise. The Apostle said there were angels around us bringing new organs, and that they would be implanted in people, and I received that word for us. Standing next to Apostle Maldonado, I saw a silhouette of fire coming toward us. When it stood in front of me, I saw it had an enormous and brilliant hand, and I heard a voice telling me to open my left hand. As I did, I saw a whirlwind going from the angel's hand toward mine. Then the angel said, "Put your hand on your wife's head." When I obeyed, I felt fire flowing

from my hand, and I could clearly feel the hole in her brain being filled. She left the CAP event completely healed.

When we went back to the hospital, the doctors said her condition could have been fatal, due to all the days in which she'd had internal bleeding. But God preserved her life, and He worked a creative miracle in her brain. We know Christ is alive and He has power.

2

A HOUSE OF PRAYER

"For My house shall be called a house of prayer for all nations."
—Isaiah 56:7

Jesus's Passion for Prayer

*J*esus was passionate about prayer. The week before He was crucified, He triumphantly entered Jerusalem, with crowds of people accompanying Him, praising God. Yet when He went to the temple—what was supposed to be the center of worship and prayer—what a contrast! It had been turned into a corrupt marketplace by those seeking to make money by selling animals to people for their sacrifices. How did Jesus respond to this? He was angered by what the temple had become, and He *"drove out all those who bought and sold in the temple, and overturned the tables of the money changers and the seats of those* *who sold doves*" (Matthew 21:12). Quoting the prophets Isaiah and Jeremiah, "*He said to them, 'It is written, "My house shall be called a house of prayer," but you have made it a "den of thieves"'*" (Matthew 21:13; see Isaiah 56:7; Jeremiah 7:11).

After Jesus rose from the dead and ascended to heaven, He sent the Holy Spirit to live within all who believed in Him. This made the corporate church, as well as individual believers, into a living temple of God. The same is the case today. As the apostle Paul wrote:

> *For you are the temple of the living God. As God has said: "I will dwell in them and walk among them. I will be their God, and they shall be My people."* (2 Corinthians 6:16)

> *Do you not know that your body is the temple of the Holy Spirit who is in you, whom you have from God, and you are not your own? For you were bought at a price; therefore glorify God in your body and in your spirit, which are God's.* (1 Corinthians 6:19–20)

As the living temple of God, the church is to be "a house of prayer." Do you have the same passion for prayer that Jesus did?

The Early Church's Passion for Prayer

The early church was characterized by this passion for prayer. The Scripture says that as Jesus's followers were waiting for the *"Promise of the Father"* (Acts 1:4)—the gift of the Holy Spirit—they gathered in an upper room and *"with one accord continued stedfastly in prayer"* (Acts 1:14 ASV). After Pentecost, as God added to the church those who were being saved, Christians *"continued steadfastly in the apostles' doctrine and fellowship, in the breaking of bread, and in prayers"* (Acts 2:42).

The church asked God for direction before making important decisions (see, for example, Acts 1:24–26) and for boldness to testify about Christ (see Acts 4:29–31). Prayer was a fundamental part of their ministry, as we can see in many biblical passages. (See, for example, Acts 2:46–47; 3:1; 6:4.) As a result, there was much spiritual life and activity in the church, with healings and miracles and deliverances.

The centrality—and power—of prayer have been lost in the church today. Churches are used for many activities, and even though these activities may be good, they are not the main purpose of the body of Christ. For example, the house of God is not a place of entertainment or even a social welfare institution or a hospital. Although activities and programs related to these purposes take place, they are not the reason why the church exists.

The church is meant to be a place of prayer, but in reality, very few congregations practice this truth. Many believers are willing to attend the Sunday morning service—but not the prayer service. They remember to pray only when they have a great need, and since they don't really know how to pray, they depend on the prayers of others.

> A life without prayer lacks spiritual activity.

You Can Be a House of Prayer

If you are among those who do not know how to pray, and who often need to depend on the prayers of others, you can become a house of prayer. This book will show you what prayer is—and how to pray. Jesus's disciples weren't sure how to pray, either, and that's why He had to teach them.

Now it came to pass, as He was praying in a certain place, when
He ceased, that one of His disciples said to Him, "Lord, teach us
to pray, as John also taught his disciples."   (Luke 11:1)

Jesus proceeded to give them a model for prayer. (See verses 2–4.)
He brought them the revelation of how to pray in a new way that
acknowledged their heavenly Father, His kingdom, and their brothers and sisters. It is crucial for the church, as the body of Christ, to
be restored to its original purpose, and to recover its true function.
When we don't have a consistent and continual prayer life, we become
spiritually weak and lazy, until we finally dry up. If you as a believer
are not passionate about being in the presence of God, something is
seriously wrong. It is clear that Jesus was passionate about prayer.
Zeal for the house of God consumed Him (see John 2:13–17); that is
why He couldn't stand seeing His Father's house turned into a mere
market. Our Lord's passion for prayer continues to this day, as *"He*
is also able to save to the uttermost those who come to God through Him,
*since **He always lives to make intercession for them**"* (Hebrews 7:25).

God's Original Intention for the Church

We can see that God's original intention for the church was
that it be a house of prayer. One of the reasons why many believers
who love God and want to please Him and do His will don't make
their churches houses of prayer is that they haven't understood
this original purpose. Our heavenly Father is calling us to return
to this essential role. Jesus is still saying to us through the voice of
the prophet Isaiah,

Even them I will bring to My holy mountain, and make them
joyful in My house of prayer. Their burnt offerings and their sac-
rifices will be accepted on My altar; for My house shall be called a
house of prayer for all nations.   (Isaiah 56:7)

I have identified five basic characteristics of a true house of God: it is a house (1) of prayer; (2) of offerings; (3) of sacrifices; (4) with a functioning altar; (5) for all nations. Besides being a house of prayer, the other four qualities must be present in the church. Let us look at each one of them and how they interconnect.

1. A House of Prayer

Once again, to be able to carry the presence and blessing of God in our lives, we need to pray continually. Such "prayer without ceasing" (see 1 Thessalonians 5:17) must be something that arises spontaneously, prompted by the Spirit of God. When prayer begins to weaken in a church, the power of God is absent, and everything starts to crumble; then, the presence of God and the Word of God become scarce; there are no miracles or blessings, there is no salvation of souls or deliverance from spiritual bondage. The only things that are left are empty religion, routine, and traditions, void of the life of Christ.

2. A House of Offerings

In Christ, God has made every believer His priest to present spiritual sacrifices and offerings to Him. Peter wrote, *"You also, as living stones, are being built up a spiritual house, a holy priesthood, to offer up spiritual sacrifices acceptable to God through Jesus Christ"* (1 Peter 2:5), and *"You are a chosen generation, a royal priesthood, a holy nation, His own special people…"* (verse 9). The church is the place where, as priests, we present our offerings to God. A church that doesn't present offerings is not a house of God. Many pastors and leaders don't teach their congregations about giving offerings—spiritual offerings, as well as monetary ones—because they're afraid people will be offended and leave the church. However, by doing this, they turn the house of God into a house of man, and they withhold the blessings people would receive by giving to God.

3. A House of Sacrifices

As a holy priesthood, we are to draw near to God to offer sacrifices like prayer, worship, praise, intercession, and offerings. Making spiritual sacrifices often involves dying to ourselves—to our wills, our time, our pride, our ambition, the use of our finances, and so forth. A church in which the people don't offer spiritual sacrifices cannot be called a house of God, because in a house of God, the priests give sacrifices; and every time they do, they draw closer to God, and the blessings come.

> A church is not authentic if it doesn't have a priesthood that presents offerings and sacrifices to God.

After a sacrifice, there is always a blessing. Look what happened when Jesus was baptized in water as an act of submission and consecration to God the Father:

> *When all the people were baptized, it came to pass that Jesus also was baptized; and while He prayed, the heaven was opened. And the Holy Spirit descended in bodily form like a dove upon Him, and a voice came from heaven which said, "You are My beloved Son; in You I am well pleased."* (Luke 3:21–22)

The "law of sacrifice" establishes that something must die in order for something else to live. That is why every blessing starts with a sacrifice. We can see this truth in the life of every man and woman of God. If you look back on your own life, do you notice that just before every blessing you received, some type of sacrifice was made? Or that, after a sacrifice, a season of blessings began for you? In the Bible, when people made sacrifices, there were open portals from heaven for them to receive something unusual from God. (See, for example, John 1:49–51; Acts 7:54–56.) The same is true today. The portals open because of the "blood" that flows from the sacrifice. Therefore, if there is sacrifice, there will also be open heavens.

> **Spiritual sacrifices open the heavens and keep them open.**

4. A House with a Functioning Altar

From the beginning of time, the altar has always been a place where God and man could meet. It is a place where sacrifices are offered, and a reminder that without the shedding of blood, there is no forgiveness of sins. (See Hebrews 9:22.) When we make the call for salvation at King Jesus Ministry, people run to the altar; there, they pour out their hearts and publicly confess Jesus as their Lord and Savior. Jesus said, *"Whoever confesses Me before men, him I will also confess before My Father who is in heaven"* (Matthew 10:32).

However, in many churches, a modern message of "hyper-grace" has essentially shut down the altar, ceasing the giving of spiritual offerings in the house of God. I will talk more about this in chapter 3, but today, in the church as a whole, the altar has been ruined, and the fire of God is no longer burning, because sacrifices haven't been offered in a long time. The altar of the church must be rebuilt to restore it to the place it deserves in the house of God. We need to urgently repair God's altar by bringing our offerings there—giving sacrifices of praise, worshipping the one true God, calling the lost to repentance, and interceding for our families and friends.

5. A House for All Nations

A church that is not open to receive all nations and peoples is not a true house of God. If, in a congregation, prejudice and racism permeate, that is not a church, regardless of its size. God's original design for His house is not for it to be a place of segregation, but a place that welcomes all races and ethnicities, and all generations; it is for young people, adults, children, and the elderly, both men and women.

The Attitude and Spirit of Prayer

The state of our world today makes it a necessity that the house of God return to its original, primary activity of prayer. We must stand and pray that God will guard His people from all the dangers occurring daily around the world—wars, hurricanes, earthquakes, sexual immorality, homicides, kidnappings, divisiveness, and much more.

Christ is coming soon! If we know this, why have we allowed prayer in the church to diminish or become nonexistent? Church prayer services should have the purpose of crying out to the Lord for His quick return, because this is what the Spirit is saying: *"And the Spirit and the bride say, 'Come!' And let him who hears say, 'Come!'… Even so, come, Lord Jesus!"* (Revelation 22:17, 20). Paul wrote, *"Not forsaking the assembling of ourselves together, as is the manner of some, but exhorting one another, and so much the more as you see the Day approaching"* (Hebrews 10:25).

Thus, for the church to be the genuine body of Christ, it needs to be a house of prayer. And to join with other Christians to become a house of prayer, the believer must always have the attitude and spirit of prayer as a state of mind. It is not about praying only when we feel like it, but about praying continually because we know it is our primary calling and function. This way, we will always be in the presence of God. All Christians must be a house of prayer, because Christianity is about being like Christ, and He always prayed. Even today, He intercedes for us before the Father. Therefore, when you are a house of prayer, you are like Christ.

> To pray, we need a state of mind in which we are always aware of the presence of God.

A Christian who is a house of prayer meditates continually on God and His Word. Prayer is not always verbal, but it does require a specific attitude and frame of mind. If you are a house of prayer, if you live in a spirit of prayer, then you will not be guided by your emotions but by the Spirit. Even if you feel like giving up or are very discouraged, you will know that God is with you! Whether you sense it or not, you can be sure that He is always there.

> The highest level of prayer occurs when a believer becomes a house of prayer.

Activation

If you realize that you haven't understood or fulfilled the main purpose of the church—being a house of prayer—then pray the following out loud:

Loving heavenly Father, I thank You for the revelation of Your intention for the church to be a house of prayer. I ask You to forgive my ignorance and negligence of the call to prayer that You have made to me as a member of the body of Christ. I wholeheartedly repent for not going to Your house to offer sacrifices, offerings, prayer, praise, and everything else You deserve and expect to receive. Forgive me for allowing the altar in Your house to be broken down, for not offering constant sacrifices there, in order to be sanctified and live in Your presence. I ask, in the name of Jesus, that You would give me a spirit of prayer and a passion to be in Your presence and to be a house of prayer myself. I declare that the spirit of prayer that was upon Jesus here on earth comes upon me now. I receive Your grace and the power of the Holy Spirit to pray Your perfect will, so that Your presence will flow in Your house—to heal, to do miracles, and to deliver Your people from demonic oppression, negative soul ties, and a lack of forgiveness. Starting today, in the name of Jesus and in the power of the Holy Spirit, I will be a house of prayer. Amen.

Testimonies of Answered Prayer

Marriage Restoration and Deliverance from Addictions

Joshua Haber, a member of King Jesus Ministry, shared the following testimony with us:

> For seventeen years, I was lost—consuming ciga-rettes, marijuana, and alcohol; for the last four years, I was addicted to lasciviousness and compulsive gam-bling. I made two hundred thousand dollars a year, but I never had money because I could not stop gambling. I'm Jewish—in fact, I grew up a messianic Jew—but my whole family lived off gambling. I tried to stop in my own strength, but I couldn't do it.
>
> Eight months ago, I went through a very critical time in my life that produced in me a strong desire to change. I came to King Jesus and, during one of the teachings, a leader told me, "There is a part of your brain that produces addiction in you. That is not from God. Surrender it to Him, and let it go. Be filled with the presence of God." I fell on my knees and gave everything to God. Then, I heard His voice telling me, "You will be protected. You will do great things, son. Follow My path, and follow Me." In that moment, I received the baptism in the Holy Spirit and I spoke in spiritual tongues. Right there, the addiction died, and I even lost the desire to look at other women. Today, I attend a House of Peace,[2] and there I am being trained

---

2. A House of Peace refers to the home of a member of King Jesus International Ministry who opens his or her doors to receive neighbors, relatives, and friends, with the purpose of sharing the gospel of the kingdom—teaching the Word of God and imparting His power. The same anointing, supernatural power, and presence of God that are found in our main church manifest there.

to become a leader. I give thanks to God for my wife, because she prayed for me every day that I was in the world, for me to become the man God had designed, and the Lord answered her prayer. I can testify that prayer has power!

Supernatural Provision to Build a Church

Apostle Mary Wildish, from Jamaica, whose ministry is under the spiritual covering of Apostle Guillermo Maldonado, shared a powerful testimony of what God did through prayer.

After nine years of looking for a piece of land on which to build our church in Montego Bay, Jamaica, we went to see the mayor, and he told us we should look for it on the outskirts of the city. We started praying and interceding to receive God's guidance. The Lord answered and led us to a specific place, a four-acre piece of land that was available. Excited about God's answer, we presented the best offer we could, which would leave our bank accounts completely empty—but we were still twenty thousand dollars short. In June of that year, we attended the Supernatural Ministry School[3] that King Jesus Ministry hosts in Miami. There, Apostle Maldonado gave us a word from God: "Paid debts, paid debts!" We took hold of that word by faith, and we continued praying over it. When we returned to Jamaica, a person came to our office and gave us twenty thousand dollars as an offering! As if that were not enough, an extra forty-five thousand dollars appeared in one of our bank accounts, supernaturally. Thanks to prayer, God provided the funds to buy the piece of land and start building the church!

---

3. The Supernatural Ministry School gathers apostles, prophets, evangelists, pastors, teachers, and leaders of great influence from the United States and abroad. They come to be trained to act according to their calling in ministry, education, government, business, and other arenas of life.

God Provides Immigration Documents and a Business

Dyanna Romero is a member of King Jesus Ministry. She is a fashion designer who traveled from her country of birth, Colombia, South America, to the United States, seeking political asylum. Prayer was key for the completion of her immigration process, as she relates in this testimony:

Some time ago, I received a prophetic word that my designs would be in the golden runways at an international level. However, I could not travel outside the United States because I didn't have the required immigration documents. I spent ten years fighting for them; I even went to the Supreme Court, but the answer was no. A few months ago, I registered for a prayer class that Prophet Ana Maldonado was teaching at the University of the Supernatural Ministry (USM).[4] As part of the training, she asked us to write our prayer petitions and put them in a box. Full of faith, I wrote, "God, thank You for bringing me to the United States. I ask, in the mighty name of Jesus, that my immigration status is defined this year." In two weeks, the immigration office granted me political asylum! Now I can travel to any country in the world!

With this solved, and with faith, I started my business with only one thousand dollars and kept working on my designs. When I presented my business plan, my company was valued at one million dollars! I kept praying, and I submitted an application to one of the greatest fashion shows in the country, called "Corp. Expo," in Las Vegas, Nevada. People told

4. The University of the Supernatural Ministry is an extension of King Jesus International Ministry.

me they wouldn't accept me because those runways are for famous designers, but I believed God and declared I would enter the fashion world through the big door. When I presented my application and my designs, they accepted me immediately and gave me one of the best places in Corp. Expo as a renowned international designer. When we pray to God with faith, He moves mountains!

God Diverts a Hurricane from the City of Miami

In September 2017, Hurricane Irma was approaching the coast of the state of Florida in a category 5 strength, with winds of 185 mph. It became the most powerful storm in the Atlantic, generating the highest accumulated cyclone energy that has ever been recorded. It was predicted that this hurricane would go through the city of Miami from south to north, causing great destruction. The more than three million residents in its path were about to experience one of the most devastating storms in history. The hurricane's arrival was considered imminent, with the authorities and much of the media considering it a given! Many people left Miami and fled north, while the authorities evacuated the higher-risk zones.

Seeing the situation, King Jesus Ministry was activated in prayer. Intercessors, pastors, elders, and the whole congregation were in prayer alert! Other friends of the ministry around the world also joined with us in prayer. During the last prayer meeting with ministry employees before the storm was to hit, Apostle Guillermo Maldonado guided the team in prayer, asking God to divert and debilitate the hurricane.

After causing destruction in Cuba, the hurricane changed its direction—instead of going north, it turned west, moving toward the Gulf of Mexico. When it finally turned back north, it advanced parallel to the west coast of Florida, moving away from Miami. The hurricane reached land in the Florida Keys, with 130-mile-per-hour winds, equivalent to a category 4 hurricane. The eye of the storm advanced through the Gulf of Mexico and approached Marco Island, off the west coast of Florida, with winds of only 115 miles per hour, equivalent to a category 3 hurricane. It finally turned into a tropical storm.[5]

Because the people of God joined in prayer, the devastation that was expected never came. The hurricane moved away from the most populated areas and weakened until it completely dissipated. God answered our prayers and saved us from what would have been a historic tragedy! Thanks to the Lord for the power of prayer!

5. Phil Klotzbach, *Hurricane Irma Meteorological Records/Notable Facts Recap*, Colorado State University, https://webcms.colostate.edu/tropical/media/sites/111/2017/09/Hurricane-Irma-Records.pdf (accessed February 7, 2018).

3

THE PRIORITY OF PRAYER

"Continue earnestly in prayer,
being vigilant in it with thanksgiving."
—Colossians 4:2

Prayerlessness has become one of the greatest deficiencies in the Christian church. This is the main reason why numerous congregations are losing members and closing their doors. Many believers lack power, authority, spiritual activity, and the manifestation of the supernatural because they prefer to be accepted by today's society, which embraces temporal values, rather than seek God and establish a strong, intimate, and eternal relationship with Him through prayer.

Additionally, the more the church is Westernized, the less prayer it engages in. When I say "Westernized," I refer to the fact that a great number of congregations get carried away by the Western world's schools, or streams, of thought, which place reason and scientific verification above the supernatural power of God—often to the point of denying the supernatural. By doing so, the church is unknowingly fostering an open contempt for faith and the life of the Spirit.

It is clear that much of the present generation greatly underestimates the supernatural; people only adhere to what is empirically provable or seems "reasonable" to human minds. Many people either don't value prayer—or do not know *how* to pray. If we are not able to transmit the true spirit of prayer to the church, that spirit will be extinguished. Instead of congregating in a true house of God, it will be as if we are merely attending a social club or a place of entertainment, where the life of the Spirit is visibly lacking.

> The power of God that you carry will always be directly proportional to your prayer life.

Why Is Prayer Being Devalued Today?

We must understand the two principal reasons why this generation doesn't value prayer or see it as a necessity.

The Spirit of This World

The "spirit of this world" is a force that openly opposes the Holy Spirit. It includes everything that Satan introduces into the culture and the traditions of nations that move people to act against the will and purpose of God, and leads them to cultivate unbelieving and sinful behavior. The spirit of the world is opposed to the idea of a relationship with God, since it denies His existence, His power, and His capacity to work on earth. "*We know that we are of God, and the whole world lies under the sway of the wicked one*" (1 John 5:19), and that "*we have received, not the spirit of the world, but the Spirit who is from God"* (1 Corinthians 2:12).

The spirit of the world even seeks to influence the minds of believers, with the intention of keeping them from esteeming what is eternal so they will rush to obtain what is only temporary. When someone is influenced by that spirit, they won't value spiritual things, including sacrifice and the giving of offerings. They won't commit to God's original purpose for the church and their lives won't be transformed. Rather, they will focus on instant gratification and worldly pleasures; consequently, they will live outside God's law and will not rely on His love, grace, wisdom, and power.

Hyper-Grace Teaching

The second reason this generation doesn't value prayer is that many people are following a "hyper-grace" teaching, which is a false doctrine. The Bible says that we are saved by grace, through faith, not by works, so that no one can boast. (See Ephesians 2:8–9.) However, God's grace is not a license to sin; rather, grace empowers us to live a righteous life before God. (See Romans 6:1–4.) The argument raised by those who defend a hyper-grace outlook is that everything has already been paid for by Jesus on the cross, so there's nothing else we need to do in the Christian life.

This argument is a half-truth. It is true that the work of the cross is complete, but it's not true that we have no responsibilities or callings to fulfill. The first thing God gave to the church is the priesthood of believers—and one of the chief roles of a priest is to pray. (See Revelation 1:5–6; 5:9–10.) We must continue our responsibilities as priests in God's kingdom in order to enforce what Christ has won for us on the cross. Otherwise, we may not realize those benefits in our lives.

In contrast, the hyper-grace message denies the importance of spiritual sacrifices like prayer, worship, fasting, and giving offerings. Thus, it discourages the ministry of the priesthood in the church. When the priesthood is removed, the manifest presence of God leaves, because continuous spiritual sacrifices are what produce the manifestation of His presence. Therefore, when believers stop exercising their priestly ministry, the altar of God is left empty and ruined—lacking the fire of God.

Need starts when your fellowship with God breaks.

The Measure of the Church

In these end times, God is measuring the church by its prayer life. In past generations, there were people who truly knew how to pray and conduct spiritual warfare. They advanced the kingdom of God by interceding and manifesting His supernatural power. They prayed until demonic chains were broken, until mountains moved, and until they received a breakthrough. If the church does not obtain victories over sin, worldliness, and Satan, then it will lose what it has gained in the Spirit.

The coming of the Lord is connected with the restoration of the end-times priesthood.

Jesus saw prayer as a spiritual necessity—equivalent to our physical need for oxygen! Just as we cannot live without air, we have no spiritual life without prayer. That is why, while Jesus was teaching His disciples, *"He spoke a parable to them, that men always ought to pray and not lose heart"* (Luke 18:1). Most people don't know the value of prayer until they find themselves in a situation that cannot be solved by natural means. However, our motivation for praying should not be our need, but rather our love for God. The truth is, we shouldn't pray only when we face impossible circumstances. Praying is communicating with God, and the Bible tells us to pray at all times (see Ephesians 6:18) and *"without ceasing"* (1 Thessalonians 5:17).

What Is True Prayer?

Prayer is two-way communication—it is a dialogue through which we speak to God and listen to Him—generating a relationship in the now, one that is present and continuous. Our communication with our heavenly Father gives life to our relationship with Him. When this communication ceases, we stop advancing in our knowledge of Him. At that point, we start merely assuming things about Him, because we have set aside our way of knowing Him. Our lack of communication disconnects us from the Lord, and the relationship begins to die. Moreover, even if we talk to God all the time, if we don't take the time to *listen* to what He is saying, we are not really praying, either, because we are really just speaking a monologue.

Communication with God is not based so much on what we say, but on what we hear from Him. And we can hear our heavenly Father only when we have a close, intimate, face-to-face relationship with Him. Certain people claim to hear God, but the fruit of their intimacy with Him is almost nonexistent. *"By their fruits you will know them"* (Matthew 7:20).

> The proof of having heard from God
> are the fruits that manifest His power,
> His love, and a radical change in our hearts.

Is it possible to have such a close relationship with God? Yes, it is possible—and God wants you to have it! But this is not something that happens immediately. Like any relationship, it must be cultivated for it to grow. The first thing a Christian must do to develop a close relationship with God is to give priority to communication with Him.

In fact, the kingdom of God is built upon the structure of relationship. This means our interactions with God can't be mechanical; they can't be based on a formula or a ritual. It is impossible to pray from a position that is not a place of relationship. Jesus said, *"If you abide in Me, and My words abide in you, you will ask what you desire, and it shall be done for you"* (John 15:7). He came to teach us a *relational theology*, so that we would be able to draw near to God without reserve. He demonstrated this purpose at the very moment of His death on the cross, when the veil of the temple was torn from top to bottom. (See Matthew 27:50–51; Mark 15:37–38.) Until then, this veil had prohibited people from entering the Holy of Holies, with the exception of the high priest, who could enter only once a year on the Day of Atonement. The tearing of the veil by heaven signified that from that moment, the way to the presence of God would remain open forever. Since that time, cultivating a relationship with God through continual communication has been the responsibility of the believer.

> **Prayer is relational and leads us to have communion with God.**

Many people have needs only God can meet, but they don't want to bother with establishing a relationship with Him; consequently, they treat Him like a "miracle vending machine." They just want to put in their "money" and have what they desire dispensed to them. But God doesn't work like that. On certain occasions, because of His mercy, He will respond to people's prayers regardless of whether they have a close relationship with Him; but it is likely that the next time they seek Him for something, He will not respond. More than meeting needs, He wants to have a continuing relationship with us. For this reason, Jesus's beloved disciple wrote, *"That which we have seen and heard we declare to you, that you also may have fellowship with us; and truly our fellowship is with the Father and with His Son Jesus Christ"* (1 John 1:3). If the relationship exists, God will take care of all our needs.

The life of Jesus is an example of continuous prayer:

Now in the morning, having risen a long while before daylight, He went out and departed to a solitary place; and there He prayed.
(Mark 1:35)

Prayer kept Jesus in a close relationship with His Father. Accordingly, all of Jesus's miracles flowed from His prayer life. Jesus knew that the Father wouldn't leave any of His Son's prayers unanswered. (See, for example, John 11:42.) It will be the same for you, if you continually maintain a relationship with God; all your needs will be supplied and you will not lack anything. The day we finally understand the true value of prayer, we will reach a point where all our prayers will be answered by God.

> Prayer was the means by which Jesus, as a Man, always stayed close to the Father.

The Purpose of Prayer

The body of Christ must complete a cycle initiated the moment the church was established by Jesus—one that will continue until the day He returns for His bride. That cycle started with "watching and praying" (see, for example, Mark 13:33), and it will close with watching and praying. Today, God is restoring the prayer mantle upon the church for the purpose of preparing us for the challenges we will face in the end times, and to enable us to be ready when Christ returns. As we have seen, prayer is surrender, sacrifice, and consecration. Through prayer, God not only wants to bless us, He also wants to transform us!

Before we move on to our next theme of prayer in chapter 4, let's review three main ways that prayer has value in the life of the believer.

1. Prayer Is the Way We Develop Our Relationship with God

Most believers don't value prayer because they don't have a close relationship with God. Prayer is the way by which we come to establish, maintain, and deepen our intimacy with the Father. Intimacy takes place when we know God, and when He holds a place in our heart. Prayer and intimacy—one depends on the other, producing a circle of blessing.

Our relationship with God also affects our human relationships.

If we walk in the light as He is in the light, we have fellowship with one another, and the blood of Jesus Christ His Son cleanses us from all sin. (1 John 1:7)

If our relationship with God is good, the rest of our relationships will also be good—and vice versa. Walking continuously in the light produces constant fellowship with that light, which is Jesus. This means that if we don't walk in fellowship, we will walk in darkness.

The way we treat people is the way we will treat God; and the way we love God is the way we will love people. For this reason, before we go into the presence of the Lord, we must make sure we are in harmony with our brothers and sisters. If, in our heart, there are resentment, unforgiveness, and offenses against other people, we must forgive them; otherwise, God won't listen to our prayers, because we will be in darkness. Jesus Himself teaches us that, if we do not forgive others their offenses, our Father who is in heaven will not forgive our offenses. (See, for example, Matthew 6:15; Mark 11:26.)

> Every other relationship is characterized by our relationship with God.

2. Prayer Prepares Us for the Second Coming of Christ

His second coming is the primary reason why Jesus commanded His church to keep "watching and praying." In Mark 13:33, He expressed this urgent need: *"Take heed, watch and pray; for you do not know when the time is."* When the church doesn't pray, it is telling Jesus it doesn't want to be united with Him in His second coming; it is revealing that it doesn't believe this will happen, and that it has chosen to ignore the value of prayer regarding this momentous event.

3. Prayer Is the Way by Which the Supernatural Comes into This World

We have seen that every one of Jesus's miracles was directly or indirectly related to His prayer life. To resurrect Lazarus, He only needed to thank the Father, which reveals the level of His communion with God. Note these words of Jesus:

> *"Father, I thank You that You have heard Me. And I know that You always hear Me, but because of the people who are standing by I said this, that they may believe that You sent Me." Now when He had said these things, He cried with a loud voice, "Lazarus, come forth!"* (John 11:41–43)

Once more, we see that Jesus did not pray at the moment of urgency; instead, He appealed to His constant prayer life to give the command that would produce the miracle. In the same way, for the church to be able to move in the supernatural, it must have a continuous prayer life.

Prayer is the way through which the supernatural moves. For the church to continue being supernatural, it must maintain a life of prayer.

Our Number One Priority

A relationship with God that doesn't include intimacy and quality time with Him is superfluous and based on our convenience alone. We must put our fellowship with Him first in our lives. He wants our total, undivided attention. In today's world, we are often so busy doing things that we forget that our relationship with God is more important than anything else. We are so occupied even with ministry activities—praying for people, meeting people's physical needs, and so forth—that we forget that our number one priority is our time with Him. Jesus is calling us to have a close relationship with the Father.

Great judgment is coming upon the earth, and we must be ready for Christ's soon return. We must go back to prayer! We must renew our communion with God!

To develop a close relationship with God, we must invest quality time in prayer.

Activation

Beloved reader, if you have been influenced by the spirit of this world, if you have abandoned your spiritual priesthood or lost your relationship with God, I invite you to say the following prayer out loud:

Gracious heavenly Father, I come before You recognizing that prayer has not been a priority in my life. I have allowed myself to be absorbed by the spirit of this world in such a way that I have abandoned the priesthood You have called me to, and I have not offered spiritual sacrifices at Your altar. My relationship with You is not what it should be; I am not growing in my knowledge of You, Your love, or Your power. I repent and ask for Your forgiveness. Even more, I ask You to renew in me a passion for prayer. I renounce the spirit of this world, in the name of Jesus, and I make the decision to seek You in prayer and to have continuous intimacy with You. You are the God of my salvation. I want to love You and be loved by You in the intimacy of prayer; I want to hear Your voice and speak to You, and to have a flow of communication between us. From now on, I retake my priesthood and commit to bringing offerings and sacrifices of prayer, worship, and obedience to Your heavenly altar, so that Your fire will descend and Your presence abide in me in a permanent way. I make a commitment to daily pray before You without distractions or interruptions, with the goal of praying one hour every day. I thank You for this new opportunity. I know I will see Your glory and power! Amen!

Testimonies of Breakthrough Prayer

A Church Is Supernaturally Protected from a Fire

David Miller is a pastor in the city of Methuen, Massachusetts, United States. His testimony about the power of prayer is amazing:

> Before we arrived in the city of Methuen, several churches had been destroyed by arson and others had closed. We worked hard to build a church, but after three years of struggle, we were determined to give up and leave. One day, my wife showed me a video of Apostle Guillermo Maldonado teaching; I watched it for five minutes and then told her, "Look for some airplane tickets. We have to go to that church." We arrived during CAP [the Apostolic and Prophetic Conference that the ministry holds every year]. When the apostle was preaching about the glory of God, my wife and I fell under that glory and spent more than three hours crying, touched by God.
>
> The next thing we did was to participate in an intensive training at the ministry's University of the Supernatural, where we received more than we expected. What impacted us the most was the intercession! When we went home again, we gathered the leadership and some volunteers and formed an intercession group. We organized a month of training, but before the training was completed, something spoke to my spirit and said, "You have to start interceding." Without a logical explanation, I obeyed, and, for the first time in our church, we got together to intercede in the early morning. When we were about to leave, I

heard that inner voice again, telling me, "Do not leave without praying around the building." And so we did that. The building houses two churches; we are on one side, and another church is on the other side. That night, someone entered the building, poured gasoline, and started a fire. The next day, we found the place full of police and firemen. It was chaos! But, miraculously, our part of the building was intact! Not even the carpet, full of gasoline, where the fire had started, was burned. Astonished, we gave thanks to God because we understood that prayer had protected the building.

A month later, the authorities still didn't know who had started the fire. An investigator called me and asked if I had any idea who might have done it. The same voice that led us to intercede told me, "Tell the investigator that the one who did this is part of the other church." I told him, and the next day, they had the person in custody. It is very important to live in the spirit of prayer. Something I have learned from Apostle Maldonado is that Jesus "spent hours in prayer and minutes with men." That is the model we are following now, and we are seeing the power of God!

Delivered from Satanism and Sexual Abuse

Kenya Guevara was born in El Salvador, Central America, nineteen years ago, and became a gang leader and satanist. Now, she is part of King Jesus Ministry. This is her testimony:

My parents emigrated to the United States when I was a small girl, leaving me in El Salvador with my father's brother. That uncle sexually abused me from the time I was six or seven years old. He would drug me and do everything he wanted with me. I felt great pain. Since I did not have any friends or anyone who could counsel me, I joined a gang with the promise that I would be okay, that the pain and the loneliness would stop. I had joined a *mara*,[6] where they forced me to do horrible things, including participate in satanism, where they marked one of my hands and led me to do a pact with the devil. It was then that I started experiencing demonic attacks; I felt that demons were observing me and chasing me. However, I know that during that time, my mom was praying for me.

Finally, the United States government gave me humanitarian asylum because of the sexual abuse I had suffered since I was a small girl, and I moved to this country. I didn't want anything to do with God, but the couple who are now my mentors[7] at church continually prayed with my mom. They never got tired of praying! Suddenly, I began sensing something changing in me; I started feeling that my hatred toward God was leaving me. One day, they invited me to a healing and deliverance retreat; as they were ministering to me, I started screaming because I felt like

6. In El Salvador, the word *mara* refers to a youth gang of violent behavior.
7. At King Jesus Ministry, a mentor is the leader of a group of disciples.

I was burning. Also, it was as if something was being ripped from within me. That day, I started asking God for an encounter with Him. I had felt Him, I knew He existed, but now I wanted an encounter. In a House of Peace, God spoke to me and said, "I am your Father." At that moment, I felt as if I was going to faint, and I started to see myself in another world. I saw myself with God, and I heard Him telling me, "I was always there with you; I never left you. You are My daughter; you won't lack anything." And I felt Him hugging me.

Now I'm another person; there are no traces of the Kenya from years ago. My life is completely different. Before, I only felt pain, but now I live in total happiness. Everything I went through and the things I did, all the knowledge and experiences from the past, I use today to evangelize and pray for youth who are going through the same circumstances I did—or worse. I have authority to tell them that God can change their lives, because He changed mine.

4

THE GOLDEN RULE OF PRAYER

"He who comes to God must believe that He is, and that He is a
rewarder of those who diligently seek Him."
—Hebrews 11:6

During the three and a half years that Jesus's disciples walked with their Master, there were at least two important spiritual matters they couldn't completely understand. One, as noted earlier, was prayer, so the disciples asked Jesus to teach them to pray. The other was faith. These same matters are stumbling blocks for the church in the present century.

Jesus asked His disciples, *"When the Son of Man comes, will He really find faith on the earth?"* (Luke 18:8). This verse seems to summarize an uncertainty that has existed since the days the Son of God walked on the earth. And the concern is valid because we see that, as the time of His second coming draws closer, evil and lawlessness are increasing on the earth and many people are abandoning their churches to join the world's ranks. Thus, when Jesus returns, genuine faith will be like currency in scarce circulation. Many have abandoned their faith in Christ at a time when we require a "mega-faith" to face the days to come.

Thus, faith and prayer must go together, yet both are rare today. If we combine their scarcity with a lack of love, the situation becomes truly serious. The Bible warns us, *"And because lawlessness will abound, the love of many will grow cold"* (Matthew 24:12). You may ask, "What does prayer have to do with love?" As we have seen, prayer is an activity that takes place within a personal relationship, based on the love that exists between God and His people. The Bible indicates that, as the end time approaches, prayer will increasingly be in jeopardy—in other words, the relationship of love that unites people with God will weaken.

This concern motivated the demand that Jesus made of the church of Ephesus when He said:

> *You have persevered and have patience, and have labored for My name's sake and have not become weary. Nevertheless, I have this against you, that you have left your first love. Remember therefore from where you have fallen; repent and do the first works, or else I will come to you quickly and remove your lampstand from its place—unless you repent.* (Revelation 2:3–5)

The times in which we are living require a greater level of faith and prayer because the forces of hell that now move on earth are of a higher level. There is a clash of supernatural forces in the second heaven, which is the sphere of principalities and powers. Evil spirits that have never before been on earth are being released from hell, which is why the darkness is getting more dense. To bind and cast out those spirits will require a greater level of power and authority—and that can only be achieved as the church becomes a true house of prayer.

Unfortunately, the modern church doesn't teach people how to pray, because it has lost the practice and experience of prayer. The spiritual world, like the natural, is governed by laws. The spiritual world is invisible; but while it can't be seen with our physical eyes, it is more real than the natural, and it's governed by its own laws. To ignore or disregard these laws can make our prayers ineffective. When we have a revelation and understanding of supernatural laws in the spiritual realm, we will have a more powerful and effective prayer life. Whoever moves continually in revelation will operate according to these greater laws.

This means that to walk in the supernatural realm, we must have revelation of what to pray and how to pray. Jesus gave a momentous revelation of what we are to pray when He taught His disciples to pray, *"Our Father in heaven, hallowed be Your name. Your kingdom come. Your will be done on earth as it is in heaven"* (Luke 11:2). These are our matters of first concern in prayer.

Prayer elevates us beyond time, space, and matter.

Prayer that is effective is made from heaven to earth, not from earth to heaven. This is sometimes known as "the prayer of the third day," in reference to the resurrection of Christ and our place in Him. It is about transcending to our position as sons and daughters of God, seated together with Christ in *"heavenly places"* (Ephesians 2:6), above principalities and powers (see Ephesians 1:20–22; 6:12), and from there, praying toward the earth. This type of prayer challenges natural laws and surpasses our physical reality; in this way, it places us above any bad medical report, family problem, monetary crisis, unemployment situation, or other negative circumstance we may be facing. Prayer elevates us to decree from a higher realm. That is why, after we pray, we are released from fear and anxiety, and we are filled with faith, knowing God is working in and through us.

> Our prayers must be such that they cause us to transcend the temporary and enter the eternal.

When we pray from our seat of authority in heavenly places, whatever fearful, doubtful, or critical things anyone else says about our situation do not matter. From that place, problems are not true reality but simple "facts" that can change according to what we decree in prayer. Why? Because when we pray, we establish the will of God with authority from a superior realm. The eternal realm determines what happens in the temporary realm. It is worth clarifying that this is not about a denial of reality or about irresponsible escapism, much less about the mechanical repetition of a mantra to obtain a desired result. It is about looking at things from the perspective of God, who has the power to change our circumstances.

Doctors don't have the power to directly change a health condition or situation. They might be able to prescribe medicine or therapy that brings a cure. Mostly, however, they can only treat the physical symptoms of problems whose origin is, more often than not, spiritual—whether from the fallen human condition, generational sin, or individual sin. Medicine will never get to the root of a problem that is anchored to a heart flooded with sin. (See Jeremiah 17:9; Matthew 15:18–19.) Yet *prayer does have the power* to deal with root issues and transform reality.

> The first breakthrough in prayer is to transcend our own reality.

Every time we decree from the position of authority where we are seated together with Christ in the heavenly realms, and pray from a position of righteousness (we will focus on this in the next chapter), it is easier to walk by faith and not by sight. (See 2 Corinthians 5:7.) We don't see the situation from a natural perspective anymore. The Spirit leads us to worship God and to declare that our miracle is complete, because in eternity, every miracle has already been supplied at the cross of Christ. Therefore, visualize yourself standing before God in heaven, having been justified by your faith in Christ. (See, for example, Galatians 2:16; 3:24.) In this place, God becomes the object of your attention and worship, and this leads you to transcend earthly reality. Being situated above the temporal realm, you now see everything from a heavenly viewpoint.

"While we do not look at the things which are seen, but at the things which are not seen. For the things which are seen are temporary, but the things which are not seen are eternal" (2 Corinthians 4:18). In this verse, human frailty is essentially contrasted with the demonstration of God's power. Human circumstances are not eternal but merely temporary. In contrast, our worship of God is eternal and thus has supremacy over any temporary situation. Once again, when we pray, we are lifted above all problems.

> When you focus on praising and worshipping God, He takes charge of your difficulties and deals with your enemies.

The Golden Rule of Prayer

This brings us to the "golden rule of prayer," which is that prayer begins when we believe in and acknowledge God's existence and qualities. The "law of faith" establishes that we cannot believe in something if we are not certain such a thing exists. Accordingly, we can't believe in God if we don't know that He is real. Scripture clarifies that "*without faith it is impossible to please Him, for he who comes to God must believe that He is, and that He is a rewarder of those who diligently seek Him*" (Hebrews 11:6). When we pray, we are affirming our belief that God is real and is available for us, here and now. The fact that we pray to Him, and He answers, confirms that God is there "*and that He is a rewarder of those who diligently seek Him.*"

> Prayer starts by recognizing God's existence and qualities. This is the golden rule of prayer.

Through faith, we believe in the existence of God and in the reality of the invisible realm. Then, through prayer, we affirm our belief, because if God didn't exist, there would be no reason to pray to Him. The origin of our prayers is thus God Himself. Only fools deny His existence (see Psalm 14:1), but God doesn't expect anyone to believe in what they don't know. We believe in God because He exists and has revealed Himself to us. Everything between God and man begins with the knowledge of Him. Jesus said,

> *In this manner, therefore, pray: Our Father in heaven, hallowed be Your name.*   (Matthew 6:9)

In other Bible versions, the word "*hallowed*" is translated "holy," "sanctified," or "honored." We begin to receive the revelation of prayer when we affirm or recognize the holiness of God and give Him honor, because He is worthy to receive our adoration. We cannot just enter His presence and immediately give Him our list of petitions. No petition should be brought before the throne of God unless we first recognize His existence and honor Him for who He is. In accordance with the golden rule of prayer, we must acknowledge the Lord as Almighty God, Holy One, everlasting Father, King of Kings, Lord of Lords, and the great I Am.

> When we pray, we affirm that God is alive and is with us and in us.

When we don't take time to affirm and honor God, we are in violation of this golden rule of prayer. What does our affirmation do? It recognizes and declares that no one can put limits on the eternal God. *"God is not a man, that He should lie, nor a son of man, that He should repent. Has He said, and will He not do?"* (Numbers 23:19). It is written in the Scriptures that God is not a man! Therefore, we should never think of Him and His capabilities in human terms. He is the highest authority in heaven and on earth. He is our Creator and Father, a supreme Being with supernatural abilities, who requires that we worship Him *"in spirit and truth"* (John 4:23–24).

Many people tend to believe that God is a distant Being, living far from them. One reason they believe this is that, in the Old Testament, God revealed Himself only outside of human beings because, after the fall of mankind, He no longer dwelled within people. The case of Moses is just one example. When God called Moses, He spoke to him from a burning bush (see Exodus 3:1–4); later, when Moses asked to see God's glory, he could only glimpse His *"back"* (see Exodus 33:18–23). As tremendous as this experience must have been, Moses never had a revelation of God living inside of him.

Today, many Christians believe that God is similarly beyond their reach, but man's relationship with the Father changed after Jesus's death and resurrection and the gift of the Holy Spirit. The good news is that God now lives within His people by His Spirit. This was one of the purposes of the work of Christ on the cross. Although Moses never had the revelation of God living inside of him, he still spoke with God as a friend. (See Exodus 33:11.) How much more can we know the Lord as our Friend through the Spirit? Remember that when Jesus died, the veil of the temple separating God from man was torn in two. Since then, those who believe in Him and have received Him into their lives have free access to God's presence, anytime and from any place.

> If you don't first affirm God in prayer,
> you will not be able to hear from Him,
> and you will not know what to pray; as a result,
> everything you pray will be on an illegal basis.

How to Affirm and Honor God

God cannot move on our behalf in any area of our lives in which we have not affirmed and honored Him. Let's begin to honor Him with our whole life. For example, how do we affirm and honor Him with our finances? Every time we give Him our tithes and offerings, we are acknowledging that He exercises lordship in the area of our money and that He is the ultimate source of our provision.

> If you don't affirm God, you don't know who He really is. Honor is the manifestation of our affirmation.

One way we affirm and honor God is through praise, which consists of recognizing His great works, His power, His mercy, His greatness, His majesty, and His supremacy above any other "god." We could say that praise is a way of boasting about Him, of showing we're proud of Him. When we praise God, we're declaring what He has done, is doing, and will do on behalf of His children. During praise, great supernatural manifestations take place, because when we affirm God, He confirms our faith in Him.

> Praise affirms the works of God, and worship affirms His Person.

Another way to affirm and honor God is through worship. We can't have a genuine relationship with Him without worshipping Him. Through worship, we acknowledge that God is present with us. We feel His presence, and we surrender to Him; we fall prostrate before Him and give ourselves to Him completely. We worship Him because He is worthy to receive our adoration. During worship, in the Spirit, we unite with the choir of the twenty-four elders who prostrate themselves *"before Him who sits on the throne and worship Him who lives forever and ever…, saying: 'You are worthy, O Lord, to receive glory and honor and power; for You created all things, and by Your will they exist and were created'"* (Revelation 4:10–11).

> The consummation of our worship is the manifestation of His presence.

Activation

Dear reader, as we conclude this chapter, I want to assist you in your prayer life by demonstrating my own practice of following the golden rule of prayer. Every day, as I present myself before the Father, I never start with personal petitions, begging for blessings, or even asking for forgiveness. I always begin by affirming and honoring Him. That doesn't mean I don't have needs or reasons to ask for forgiveness, but I know that I must first acknowledge Him as Lord in all the areas of my life. I do this freely, in whatever way the Spirit leads me, in this manner:

> Heavenly Father, You are my source of life, of salvation, and of provision. You are the great I Am, eternal and immeasurable, the One who has life in Himself. You are almighty and fearsome. I remove the limitations in my mind so You can do Your will and perform miracles and wonders in me and through me. I worship You as my Healer, because You carried my diseases at the cross. Thank You for being a merciful, faithful, good, and righteous God.

After I affirm the Lord, I ask Him for forgiveness for whatever I need to. In this way, I can stand in a position of righteousness to declare the miracles that Jesus released at the cross, which I need to establish on earth to keep expanding His kingdom.

This is what I do—now, you go and do the same!

Testimonies of Breakthrough Prayer

A Young Man Is Healed of Leprosy

Sergio is twenty-seven years old and a member of King Jesus Ministry in Maryland, United States. Before he met Christ, he was suffering from leprosy. The disease was consuming him—he had many sores, his torso was raw, and the skin on his hands and legs was ripped. Because of this condition, he had once tried to commit suicide twice in a single day. But when he had an encounter with the Lord, the leprosy instantly disappeared from his body! Here is his testimony:

My family used to practice witchcraft, and the disease of leprosy came into my life as part of a curse. I lost all hope; I couldn't see a reason to live if I had to live like that. When I showered, I bled a lot because my skin would tear. I had to spend days in the hospital. During this time, my friends left me; not even my parents or my uncles would visit me. I was completely alone. The doctors told me I would continue to suffer this disease for more than a year.

When I couldn't take it anymore, in the middle of the night, I cried out to God. I acknowledged Him as the only and supreme God, Creator of the universe and of my life. Then He revealed Himself to me and gave me strength, and I was able to get up from bed. I broke the pact my family had with Satan and made a new covenant of faithfulness to Christ. His blood cleansed me, and all the signs of leprosy disappeared. Today, I ask Him to help me persevere, regardless of the trial I may be facing. I serve Him, and I am a living testimony of His power.

Affirming and honoring God activated the power of the cross in Sergio's life! Glory to the Lord!

A Son Is Restored to His Family

Pastor Diana Nunez is part of my ministerial team at King Jesus Ministry. I train all my leaders in prayer and in the supernatural, to equip them to go and do the work of the kingdom. She shared this testimony of how God worked to bring sons and daughters who were in the world back to their families:

One Sunday, while I was preaching during the 9:00 a.m. service, the Holy Spirit told me to call forward the mothers whose children had left home and were in the world. About thirty mothers walked to the altar. The Holy Spirit told me that, because of those mothers' prayers, in less than thirty days, their children would return home and to the Lord. So, I prayed accordingly and declared that this word would be fulfilled.

Weeks later, as I was walking in a hallway of the church, a woman approached me and told me she was one of the mothers whom I had ministered to that day. She had been praying for her son to return home and serve the Lord. That Sunday, she believed with all her heart what I had declared, and, in less than thirty days, she received a call from her son in which he told her he would be returning home. Days later, her son came back home; the very next Sunday, he went to church, received Christ, and was baptized in water. She testifies that her son now is completely transformed and serves the Lord!

A Woman Is Resurrected

Ruth and her husband traveled from Peru, South America, to one of our ministry events, and her husband gave this testimony:

> We found out we were expecting our second baby, and we were very happy, but complications soon arose that clouded our joy. The doctors told us the baby was at high risk. In her fifth month of pregnancy, my wife had several hemorrhages. We went to the emergency room, where we were told that the baby had already died [and would need to be surgically removed]. When they took my wife to surgery, the doctor told me there was only a 2 percent probability she would live. Immediately, I started praying, and I prayed continuously. Then, in the operating room, my wife lost two-and-a-half liters of blood and suffered respiratory failure and pulmonary obstruction. I was informed that Ruth had died on the operating table, and the doctors were doing all they could to revive her, but she wasn't responding. At that moment, our pastor connected with me and started praying, decreeing health upon her life in the name of Jesus. He declared the power of the resurrection upon her, and in that instant, my wife responded and slowly started to stabilize.
>
> Ruth says that during this time, she saw two white lights; they were like two angels telling her, "It's not your time yet." She had died, but prayer released the power of God and resurrected her. However, the crisis did not end there because, after the operation, she didn't recognize anyone, not even me or her family. She didn't even remember she had a child.

Nothing! The doctors said she had suffered damage from hypoxia, which is a lack of oxygen in the blood. They told me I had to prepare myself because Ruth wouldn't regain normalcy, and that it would be at least two years before she recovered half of her memory. But we did not give up! We started a prayer chain, and, with brothers and sisters from various parts of the country, we persevered in prayer without ceasing. Less than a month later, Ruth started to recover her memory. Less than three months after having been discharged from the hospital, she was worshipping God again at our church's altar, just as she used to do before all this happened. She doesn't have any traces of damage from the hypoxia, and she doesn't need to continue taking any pills. Our God does miracles and resurrects the dead! We should never stop praying; we should never stop believing.

5

PRAYING FROM A POSITION OF RIGHTEOUSNESS

"The effective, fervent prayer of a righteous man avails much."
—James 5:16

The first thing most people seek when they go before God in prayer is to be filled with faith. Nevertheless, even though faith is an essential element in prayer, it is not enough to assure that our prayers will be answered and that we will achieve the breakthroughs we hope for. When we pray, even more important than having faith is being in a place of righteousness. In any area where the righteousness of God does not prevail, our faith will not be sufficient, because righteousness is the seat of faith. Additionally, although God has given every person a measure of faith (see, for example, Romans 12:3, 6), there are some matters that require an extra dose of faith, and to achieve them, it is equally necessary to be standing in a place of righteousness. We can have enormous faith, but if our life is not right before God, He will not answer our prayers. Apart from righteousness, faith becomes ineffective.

> Every prayer must be offered from a place of righteousness.

This leads us to ask, who is considered righteous? It is those who remain aligned with God's nature and character through Christ. When we are not aligned with God, with His name and His Word, we become an easy prey for the enemy. It was for this reason that, at the cross of Calvary, Jesus took all our faults and sins upon Himself. The Son made us righteous before the Father—as righteous as He is! (See, for example, Romans 3:21–22.)

Jesus said, "*This is My blood of the new covenant, which is shed for many for the remission of sins*" (Matthew 26:28). To be "justified" and made righteous is to be brought back to a state of complete innocence, where every sin is erased and there is no record left of our transgressions. To be justified is to be forgiven and cleansed from all iniquity. The key to understanding righteousness and justification is the word *remission*, which means to deliver someone from the guilt or the punishment they deserve for their sin. The term reflects the definitive and perfect character of Christ's sacrifice. In essence, what it expresses is that, due to the finished work at the cross, God doesn't see us as sinners but as righteous. No human being could ever have made themselves righteous on their own; God had to send His only Son to earth to redeem us from sin.

> Our position of righteousness before God determines whether our prayers will be answered.

In any area of our lives in which we are not standing in the righteousness Jesus won for us, the enemy will have the legal right to accuse us before God. For example, if a man mistreats his wife, he won't receive an answer to his prayers in the area of family, because his position of unrighteousness will hinder his prayers. (See 1 Peter 3:7.) Likewise, if a woman does not submit to her husband, or doesn't give him his place as the head of their home, she will be in an unrighteous position before the Father. (See, for example, Ephesians 5:22–23.) In the same way, if a businessperson abuses their employees, not paying them a fair wage or respecting their rights, they won't be standing in a position of righteousness in the area of business and finances, and God will not hear their prayers. (See, for example, Colossians 4:1.) If a wealthy person steals from the poor or from widows, they are acting unjustly, and God will not answer their prayers, either. (See, for example, Isaiah 10:1–2.)

Therefore, before we ask something of God, we must examine ourselves to see if we are violating His commandments or not reflecting His nature and will. Jesus always lived in righteousness, and that is why the Father answered all His prayers. The Son continually remained in a close relationship with the Father, aligned with His perfect will. As noted earlier, that is why, when Jesus was in front of Lazarus's tomb, rather than praying for a miracle to happen, He simply gave thanks to God, saying, *"Father, I thank You that You have heard Me. And I know that You always hear Me…"* (John 11:41–42). He always prayed from a place in the Spirit in which the word *impossible* was meaningless.

"Father,…You always hear Me"! That is the level of prayer we can reach if we continually live in righteousness.

Obstacles to Praying from a Place of Righteousness

If we remove the obstacles to praying from a place of righteousness, we can be assured that our prayers will be heard by God. Here are the major barriers and how we can break these roadblocks to our relationship and communication with the Lord.

Iniquity

> *Your iniquities have separated you from your God; and your sins have hidden His face from you, so that He will not hear.*
>
> (Isaiah 59:2)

The word for *iniquity* in Hebrew indicates the bending or twisting of morality, to the point of perverting it from the roots. Iniquity is a great evil that does not allow us to walk according to the norm of the righteousness and holiness of God. The term alludes to the extreme immorality and perversity that originates in the heart of man. (See, for example, Matthew 15:18–19.) Iniquity and sin (missing the mark of obedience to God's commandments) are the two conditions that separate us from God, preventing us from being in right standing before His presence. They are the opposite of righteousness and have a greatly detrimental influence on our prayers, because God cannot live in an atmosphere of unrighteousness.

No one can pray with iniquity in their heart, because everything iniquitous is a perversion of God's ways.

God will not hear, attend to, or answer a prayer made from a place of unrighteousness. Regardless of how much we may plead, cry out, or shout, He will not hear us! For example, those who twist the truth are living in a state of dishonesty. Those who don't recognize authority and refuse to be accountable for their actions are perverting obedience. Those who harbor unforgiveness, bitterness, or hatred are distorting God's love, and their hearts are filled with rebellion. People often ask themselves, "Why doesn't God answer my prayers?" The answer to this question, for a number of people, comes from the following teaching of Jesus, which He gave while instructing His disciples about prayer: *"And whenever you stand praying, if you have anything against anyone, forgive him, that your Father in heaven may also forgive you your trespasses"* (Mark 11:25).

The Scriptures say of Satan, *"You were perfect in your ways from the day you were created, till iniquity was found in you"* (Ezekiel 28:15). Iniquity is a mixture of the carnal and the demonic, which perverts the righteousness of God. When there's dishonesty, unforgiveness, envy, lack of love, bitterness, resentment, hatred, or rebellion in us, we are not standing in a position of righteousness. Where there are corrupt mixtures and contamination—which are the opposite of purity, holiness, and alignment with the will of God—there is a heart full of iniquity. Every time a person has wrong motives or an agenda that is the opposite of God's, they are in a place of unrighteousness. To sum up, if a person perverts truth, godly submission, or love—or any combination of these—God will not hear their prayers.

To sin is to miss the mark, to transgress is to break the law, but to be iniquitous is to twist and pervert the righteousness of God.

A Guilty Conscience

One of the keys to establishing a good relationship with God is the ability to speak confidently with Him, without any feelings of guilt or condemnation. The psalmist said, *"If I regard iniquity in my heart, the Lord will not hear"* (Psalm 66:18). He was aware that guilt often comes when we feel condemnation in our hearts. The enemy is an expert at setting snares to stop us from becoming closer to God; he uses our transgressions, injustices, iniquities, or any other sins of commission or omission to accuse us, rub blame and guilt in our faces, and prevent us from praying in peace. What should we do? We must go before God with *"a broken and a contrite heart,"* acknowledge our sin, repent, and ask for forgiveness: *"The sacrifices of God are a broken spirit, a broken and a contrite heart—these, O God, You will not despise"* (Psalm 51:17). It is essential that we learn to receive God's forgiveness, through the blood of Jesus, after confessing and forsaking our sins. After we have repented, if the enemy continues to bring condemnation, we must rebuke him and command him to leave in Jesus's name.

> Guilt destroys our faith and invalidates our ability to pray.

The Word encourages us to draw close to God *"with a true heart in full assurance of faith, having our hearts sprinkled from an evil conscience and our bodies washed with pure water"* (Hebrews 10:22). If we go to God with a clean conscience, as His sons and daughters, in the name of Jesus, standing from a place of righteousness, He hears us. However, if we feel guilty—either because we have not confessed our sin or because we have not received God's forgiveness in Christ—our prayers will be blocked. Don't forget that we can never enter God's presence on the basis of our own merits, intelligence, or personal abilities, but only because we are clothed with the righteousness of God. (See, for example, Job 29:14; Isaiah 61:10.) We are righteous, and the works we perform are, too, because Christ gave us a new nature of righteousness at the cross. Knowing and living in this righteousness is the only way we can have *"boldness to enter the Holiest by the blood of Jesus"* (Hebrews 10:19).

> Feelings of condemnation are a great obstacle to having our prayers answered.

Self-Righteousness

All believers are called to be in a place of righteousness before God. We have been clothed with Christ's righteousness so *"that we might become the righteousness of God in Him"* (2 Corinthians 5:21). This means that, if Christ has made our nature righteous, then we have been empowered to do righteous works—but not because of anything we do apart from Him. Let me emphasize once more that we can't do any righteous works in our own strength, but only because we have been justified by Christ, and God's Holy Spirit lives within us. Self-righteousness has no place in our lives. Remember that you don't have to try to justify yourself to receive God's approval. When you repent of your sin and ask for forgiveness, the divine provision for justification that was completed at the cross is activated, by which the blood of Christ cleanses you and His righteousness is placed in your heart. This enables you to come boldly to the throne of God's grace and have your prayers answered.

Righteousness Captures God's Attention

God's righteousness is an aspect of His holiness. That is why righteousness and a healthy fear of God are always connected in the life of the believer. The life and reign of David are excellent examples of this truth. While David remained in the will of God, his kingdom prospered; but when David fell into sin, the foundations of righteousness and the fear of God were undermined in his life, causing a crisis that affected not only him and his family, but also Israel as a nation. However, when David sincerely repented, God forgave him because he was *"a man after His own heart"* (1 Samuel 13:14; see also Acts 13:22) who loved God and desired to do His will.

Through such examples, God teaches us that He *"is far from the wicked, but He hears the prayer of the righteous"* (Proverbs 15:29). We also learn that *"the eyes of the LORD are on the righteous, and His ears are open to their cry"* (Psalm 34:15). This is the vision you must have while you pray: the eyes of the Lord are on you, He watches over the righteous, and *"the effective, fervent prayer of a righteous man avails much"* (James 5:16). In prayer, you must capture the ear and the attention of God. If you are standing in righteousness, having been justified by the work of Christ on the cross, He will take note and hear you.

> Being in a place of righteousness, our task is to intercede for those who don't know God or who live separated from Him.

Righteousness and Mercy Go Together

In Genesis, we read that God was about to destroy Sodom and Gomorrah due to their great iniquity. However, before His judgment fell upon those two cities, the Lord communicated His intentions to Abraham, who began interceding before the throne of God. *"Abraham approached him and said: 'Will you sweep away the righteous with the wicked?'"* (Genesis 18:23 NIV). Abraham continued to stand as an intercessor, saying, *"May the Lord not be angry.... What if only ten [righteous people] can be found there?"* (verse 32 NIV). And God's answer was, *"For the sake of ten, I will not destroy it"* (verse 32 NIV). He promised this because of His love for the righteous.

Unfortunately, in these times, there are some intercessors who pray for judgment, not mercy. Instead of preventing judgment against a person, city, church, or nation, they just want God to destroy everything. That is not the heart of a righteous intercessor. That was not the heart of Jesus, nor that of the apostle Paul, who said, *"For God is my witness, whom I serve with my spirit in the gospel of His Son, that without ceasing I make mention of you always in my prayers"* (Romans 1:9).

> When we aren't living in righteousness, and we pray for the judgment of God to come against someone, judgment will come upon us.

"For judgment is without mercy to the one who has shown no mercy. Mercy triumphs over judgment" (James 2:13). I am convinced that God has stopped His judgment against many people due to the intercession of the righteous. Likewise, thanks to the prayers of righteous men and women, many have been saved from going to hell. Today, many people can testify that they are alive and reconciled to God because someone prayed for them when they were separated from the Father.

How to Walk in Righteousness

Practice Repentance as a Lifestyle

Every time we sin against God, or we allow iniquity and perversion a place in our hearts, we must repent. Repentance brings us back into the presence of God and opens the channels for Him to hear our prayers. *"He who covers his sins will not prosper, but whoever confesses and forsakes them will have mercy"* (Proverbs 28:13).

When a person has iniquity in their heart, they will always find a way to do things "their way"—meaning, separated from God! What do you plan to do apart from God? Maybe you've considered lying? Remember that once you lie, you must keep lying in order to stick with the first lie. David expressed to the Lord, *"He who works deceit shall not dwell within my house; he who tells lies shall not continue in my presence"* (Psalm 101:7). We need to pray, "Lord, if there is any sin or iniquity in me, remove it! Lead me in Your path!" (See Psalm 139:23–24.)

Repentance causes God's ear to incline to us.

Seek First the Righteousness of God

Put on the new man which was created according to God, in true righteousness and holiness. (Ephesians 4:24)

Jesus taught His disciples to seek and follow after God's righteousness. In Matthew 6:33, He said, *"But seek first the kingdom of God and His righteousness, and all these things shall be added to you."* The phrase *"seek first"* urges us to make the righteousness of the kingdom a priority. This means that, above anything else, we should always desire to be in good standing with God. We should regularly ask ourselves, "Am I right with God? Am I aligned with His will?" If we are not, we must examine ourselves and determine in which area we must repent so we won't lose our place of righteousness in His presence.

Every answered prayer is aligned with heaven. The alignment of our prayers also determines the speed of God's answer.

Always Watch and Pray

Paul exhorted the Thessalonian believers to *"pray without ceasing"* (1 Thessalonians 5:17). It is vital for believers who wish to maintain their place of righteousness to watch and be careful that their prayers do not weaken. On the contrary, we must make sure our prayer time grows and becomes the first and most important task of each day, because our relationship and fellowship with God depend on it. When we watch in the presence of God with a righteous heart, the Holy Spirit shows us any areas of unrighteousness in our lives, or where we have allowed the enemy to gain a foothold. (See Ephesians 4:27 NIV.) We must pray daily, without ceasing, because whether consciously or unconsciously, we may expose ourselves through sin and give room for the enemy to work.

> Our position of righteousness must be reaffirmed daily.

Activation

Beloved reader, I have a strong urge in my spirit to share with you more about how I go before the presence of God as my first activity every day. Let me first reaffirm what I have already said, that I don't first go before His presence with a list of petitions, but I always begin my communication with my beloved Father by worshipping and honoring Him. Neither do I start by asking for forgiveness for my faults, but by affirming Him as the Lord of my life, the Great I Am, God Almighty. Only after I enter His presence do I start confessing my faults and repenting of every sin, transgression, and unrighteousness.

Once I receive His forgiveness, I don't allow the enemy to keep accusing me of those sins, because Jesus has already erased them. I am justified by my faith in Jesus and His redeeming work on the cross; my sins have been removed by the blood of Christ, and in His name, I am empowered to do what He has commissioned me to do. If I don't feel peace, I know I need to submerge myself in God's Word, which purifies me of contamination. I ask Him to cleanse me, justify me, and sanctify me. Once I am in a place of righteousness, I know the channels for speaking with God are open. In that place, I can speak with Him face-to-face, and I feel a great certainty in my heart that He is listening to my prayers—which I make guided by the Holy Spirit, so that I don't pray anything outside of His will.

Last, I would like to share something very personal. My goal, as a son of God, is to reach the point where all my prayers are answered by my Father, just as Jesus's were. I feel this is the way the Lord wants to take each of us in the body of Christ.

Testimonies of Breakthrough Prayer

Healed of Bipolar Disorder

Mario, who is now a member of our ministry, came to us after having been diagnosed with a serious psychiatric illness that didn't allow him to have a normal life. The continuous prayers of our church produced a miracle in his life!

When I was fifteen years old, I was diagnosed with bipolar disorder type 1. The only prospect my mother had for my future was one of disability. I went through three bankruptcies because I wasn't capable of administering my finances. I even attempted to kill myself. My life had no meaning. I didn't feel capable of doing anything on my own, and I needed help for everything. Desperate, I came to King Jesus church, asking God for one more opportunity. When I started hearing revelation about our freedom in Christ through deliverance, I was able to receive healing. Once I was delivered, I began to grow as I followed the church's discipleship program. Today, I am the leader of a House of Peace, where people are filled with the presence of God and are delivered by His power. My life has changed so much that now my mother can clearly see the fruit of what God has done in me. She was even able to retire and receive some rest, because now I am capable of looking after her business. I'm actually the owner and director of the company she formed.

Thank God for the prayers that, from a place of righteousness, are made in this ministry!

Delivered from Alcoholism

Jaro is a member of our ministry who has a wonderful testimony of the power that is released when a wife stands in righteousness before God.

I gave my life to Christ when I was eight years old, but I walked away from His ways and ended up falling into alcoholism. I drank every day—so much so that, one day, God told me to choose between His kingdom and the one I was drowning in; He said that would be my last opportunity to repent. My wife was part of King Jesus church, and as she started growing spiritually, she began to seek God in different ways— through morning prayer, discipleship, and tabernacle meetings. One day, similar to what God had done, she gave me an ultimatum. My daughters were suffering, and my life was in chaos!

I remember that the more I would drown in sin, the more my wife would become involved in the vision of the church and in prayer. Then, one of my drink mates died, and I felt it had been my fault. When I went to the morgue to identify his body, I broke down and asked God to help me. About the same time, God revealed Himself to me in a dream and showed me He would accelerate my spiritual life and that I would serve Him alone. One morning, during a deliverance retreat, God transformed me, and since then, I haven't been the same person. That morning, I promised God I would serve Him for the rest of my days.

Many times, the enemy tries to bring people into our lives who claim to be our friends, but now I recognize that real friendship is found only in Jesus

Christ. If you give your marriage to Him, He will restore it; if you give Him your finances, He will multiply them. Today, I can testify that God transformed my life, restored my home, and doubled my finances! Additionally, I have my own car repair shop. Now, just as others prayed for me, I stand in righteousness and pray for men who are struggling with alcoholism, so that God is glorified by doing in them the same work He did in me.

Saved from 100 Years in Prison

Jaime is an entrepreneur who came to the feet of Christ while he was in jail, due to a prayer offered in a House of Peace connected with our ministry. His testimony shows the power of prayer given from a place of righteousness.

I owned some apartments, as well as other properties and a car business. However, my partners wanted to steal my business, and one day they planted sixty pounds [thirty kilograms] of cocaine in one of my properties. I was accused of being a drug-dealing kingpin. My lawyers said there was no way out for me because the authorities were claiming they had evidence to incarcerate me for life.

My sentence was a hundred years in prison. I was desperate; I didn't know what to do or who to go to. Everything pointed to my spending the rest of my days locked up for a crime I had not committed. But God had other plans. The manager who administered my properties told me she attended a House of Peace where they prayed and miracles happened. She promised they would pray for me. In prison, I received Jesus as the Lord and Savior of my life, and I placed all my trust in Him.

God used that House of Peace as a heavenly portal to give me back my freedom. After I spent thirty-three days in prison, God was my Justice, and the judge granted me freedom! I was not even released on bail, and the penalty was reduced to a minimum punishment to be fulfilled out of prison. I did not know about the power of prayer, but I knew my life had changed in a supernatural way. Today, I can testify that God restored my life and gave me back everything the enemy tried to steal from me. In that same House of Peace, my wife and I now serve God with profound thankfulness for what He did for me.

6

PRAYING ACCORDING TO THE WILL OF GOD

"Now this is the confidence that we have in Him, that if we ask anything according to His will, He hears us. And if we know that He hears us, whatever we ask, we know that we have the petitions that we have asked of Him."
—1 John 5:14–15

One of the fundamental purposes of prayer is that the will of God be done on earth as it is in heaven. Jesus was a Man of prayer, and what characterized His life was His strong desire to please His Father and do His will. (See, for example, Matthew 6:9–10; 26:39, 42; John 4:34.) Therefore, when someone merely prays that God would fulfill their own desires, they're showing they don't really know Him.

I have come to the place in which, in all my prayers, I long for God to manifest His will, and that is why He always answers those prayers. The Lord is not changeable in His ways, and He does not show partiality in answering people's prayers. (See Romans 2:10–11; James 1:17.) He answers the prayers of everyone who prays according to His will. We must remember that the rules on how prayers are answered are not set by the one who is asking, but by the One who has all the resources to answer each prayer according to His purposes.

> **The answers to our prayers depend on their alignment with the will of God.**

As I mentioned previously, for us to pray from heaven to earth, we have to be in unity and harmony with the Father. Accordingly, the objective of prayer is that our spirits be aligned with God's Holy Spirit, who dwells in us, so that the divine within us calls to the divine from heaven. As the Scripture says, *"Deep calls unto deep"* (Psalm 42:7). We must be aware that there is always more to receive from God than what we have experienced from Him up to this moment. In the first century, when the people of God were just being established as the church, most of their prayers concerned knowing what the will of God was because they didn't have the New Testament as we know it today, with its fuller revelation of the will of God for us in Jesus Christ. Now, our prayers must seek to accomplish His will as revealed to us by the Holy Spirit through His Word. For example, the Word teaches it is the will of God for all people to repent and be reconciled to Him. The apostle Peter wrote, *"The Lord is not slack concerning His promise, as some count slackness, but is longsuffering toward us, not willing that any should perish but that all should come to repentance"* (2 Peter 3:9).

The will of God proceeds from the mind of God, whose thoughts and instructions are made known to us in the now. Of course, the human mind is too small to contain the whole revelation of God's mind! However, the more intimate our communion with Him is, the more clearly we will understand His plans and purposes.

Ignorance Is a Spiritual Stronghold

Ignorance is a powerful mental stronghold that prevents us from knowing God's will and living in it. For this reason, the apostle Paul was led by the Holy Spirit to pray that the Colossian believers "*may be filled with the knowledge of* [God's] *will in all wisdom and spiritual understanding*" (Colossians 1:9). As we surrender our human wills to God, He will reveal His will to us, primarily through His Word and the ministry of the Holy Spirit in our lives.

> The will of God is a mystery that must be revealed in the now.

When we operate in ignorance, we can't cry out to God in a way that will bring a breakthrough. We can't claim the relevant promises if we're not aware of them—or if we're not sure they belong to us. Thus, not knowing the will of God can be highly destructive. (See, for example, Hosea 4:6.) If we want our prayers to be answered, we must know the will of God and then make sure our desires are aligned with it. Many believers become discouraged and give up when they don't see their prayers answered, because they ignore this principle.

> The greatest mental stronghold is ignorance.

What Is God's Will?

If we want to know God's will, we must first look to the finished work of Christ on the cross. There, Jesus paid the penalty for our sin, according to the purpose of the Father to reconcile mankind to Himself. Jesus's work of redemption on our behalf is complete. That is why, before He died, our Lord declared, *"It is finished!"* (John 19:30). This indicates, "All has been fulfilled," or "Everything has been paid for." What did Christ accomplish for us? He secured our salvation and set us free from all condemnation; He paid for our healing, prosperity, and transformation. His death on the cross gave us back our identity as children of God and made us joint-heirs with Christ of all His riches in glory. Additionally, He delivered us from the curse of the law, cleansed us from unrighteousness, and clothed us with His righteousness. He did all of this so that we could return to having an intimate relationship with our heavenly Father.

Knowing this, we can no longer pray, "Lord, if it's Your will...." No! The will of the Father has already been decreed and must be put into effect. We must establish it in our life, in our calling, in our ministry, and in our work. This means, for example, that if we know Jesus carried all our sicknesses, we don't have to go to God asking, "Lord, if it's Your will, heal me." We can declare what He has already decreed in His Word: "Jesus carried our sicknesses!" and "by His stripes we are healed!" (See, for example, Isaiah 53:4–5.)

The faith that comes from God is not such that we believe whatever we feel like believing, but only what is truly aligned with the will of the Father. That is why, when we pray, our first question must be, "Is this the will of God, according to His Word?" Is it the will of God for us to be healthy, free, and prosperous? Is it the will of God for a man and a woman to form a family? We can say yes to these questions because they are in accordance with what the Bible expresses. Now, it's clear that you cannot do something that is outside of God's will and expect Him to bless you. If you want to see God work in your life, you must know and establish His will, because that is the only way you will receive His blessings. Jesus said, *"Until now you have asked nothing in My name. Ask, and you will receive, that your joy may be full"* (John 16:24).

> It is not God's will to leave prayers unanswered.
> He is always ready to answer us.

The Acceleration of Prayer in the End Times

Nevertheless, we know that certain prayers have not yet been answered—including Jesus's own prayer, on the night He was arrested, that all believers be one, as He and the Father are one. (See, for example, John 17:11–26.) Why haven't these prayers been answered? The Bible teaches that, in heaven, there are *"golden bowls full of incense, which are the prayers of the saints* [believers]" (Revelation 5:8). These bowls have not yet been "poured out" on the earth in a visible or tangible manifestation of the answers. The *"saints"* that the book of Revelation mentions are located on earth, as well as in heaven. Those *"bowls"* contain the prayers of the apostles, prophets, and pastors, along with the prayers of multitudes of believers over the centuries— including your prayers. They also contain the prayers of Jesus, who continues to pray for the unity of believers. In my view, the book of Revelation is telling us that, as the church enters the end-time portion of the "watching and praying" prayer cycle, there will be an acceleration in spiritual matters, so that all prayers will be answered, because God doesn't leave any prayers unanswered.

The pouring of the bowls of incense—the prayers of the saints—is an event of the end times.

An angel has been sent to earth to accelerate the fulfillment of all prayers, before the second coming of Jesus. However, we must be aligned with God's purposes in order to participate in this end-times fulfillment of prayer. That is why a section of the model prayer Jesus taught His disciples says, "*Your kingdom come. Your will be done on earth as it is in heaven*" (Matthew 6:10). We live in times when delay has ended, when what has been prophesied will be fulfilled, and when prayers will be answered. "*Therefore say to them, 'Thus says the Lord* God: "*None of My words will be postponed any more, but the word which I speak will be done,*" *says the Lord* God'" (Ezekiel 12:28).

When Jesus's prayer for unity among believers is fulfilled, it will be the consummation of all prayers prayed according to God's will.

Four Principles for Receiving Immediate Answers to Prayer

How can we become aligned with God's purposes and receive immediate and accelerated answers to prayer? We need to know—and act on—the revelation contained in the following four principles of God's will, which will enable us to break through all spiritual stagnation:

1. Know the will of God.

2. Be in—and remain in—the will of God.

3.   Do the will of God.

4.   Speak according to the will of God.

We will explore these four truths so that you can apply them to your life and receive an answer to every prayer you have made according to the will of the Father. My greatest desire is that you may know God, renew your mind, and walk in His will.

1. Know the Will of God

The more precise we are with our prayers, the quicker the answers will come. That precision will always depend on our knowledge of the will of God. For example, if our prayers are prompted by the fleshly nature, God will not answer them, whereas, the more our prayers are guided by the Spirit, the closer we will be to the answers. God doesn't meet our whims or give us things that will harm us. His will for us is for good and not for evil, although we may not recognize or acknowledge this all the time. (See Jeremiah 29:12.) He will give us those things that are in accordance with the purpose He has placed in our lives, and that will bring the greatest blessings to us.

> *Now this is the confidence that we have in Him, that if we ask anything according to His will, He hears us. And if we know that He hears us, whatever we ask, we know that we have the petitions that we have asked of Him.*   (1 John 5:14–15)

Thus, if God hears everything we ask *"according to His will,"* then the key to making a precise prayer and to obtaining an immediate answer is to know His will. In other words, faith is "now," but whoever doesn't know the will of God will usually position their faith in the future and not in the present, with the result that the answers to their prayers will be delayed.

Faith begins where the will of God is known.

Jesus clearly knew the will of the Father. However, for an instant at Gethsemane, He struggled to surrender His will to the Father because He knew what He would have to go through to sacrifice His life for us. But, immediately, He yielded His will: *"Father, if it is Your will, take this cup away from Me; nevertheless, not My will, but Yours, be done"* (Luke 22:42). At that moment of surrender, help came from heaven, as an angel appeared to Him and gave Him strength. (See verse 43.) Many believers find it difficult to surrender their wills to God. If that is the case for you, know that in the moment you surrender your personal will, help will come. Do not fear. Abandon yourself to the will of the Father!

The will of God is not something we can know in a natural way. There is no scientific method for comprehending it. Neither does the human mind understand it instinctively. It is something the Holy Spirit reveals to us when we maintain a relationship with Him. For us to know God's will, it is first necessary to know Him as a Person. For that, we must walk with Him daily, dedicating time for intimacy with Him through prayer, as well as for reading and studying His Word.

Whoever doesn't know the will of God will easily doubt Him.

When someone knows the Lord, they know what is pleasing to Him and what is displeasing to Him. They understand what gives Him joy and what grieves Him. They're immersed in His love, and they learn to love Him in response. In such a relationship, a believer's mind is transformed, and they start to know and do God's will.

I beseech you therefore, brethren, by the mercies of God, that you present your bodies a living sacrifice, holy, acceptable to God, which is your reasonable service. And do not be conformed to this world, but be transformed by the renewing of your mind, that you may prove what is that good and acceptable and perfect will of God. (Romans 12:1–2)

We will never be able to know God's will if our mind has not been transformed and renewed. The knowledge of His will progresses in the same measure that the renewing of our mind advances. So again, to know the will of God, we must have experienced the renewing of our mind.

> The renewing of the mind is a sign of spiritual activity and of a relationship with God. Our knowledge of God's will progresses in the same measure that the renewing of our mind advances.

2. Be in—and Remain in—the Will of God

Knowing the will of God is one thing, but remaining firm in it is another. Jesus said, *"If you abide in Me, and My words abide in you, you will ask what you desire, and it shall be done for you"* (John 15:7). To remain in the Lord is to walk in His will. To do this, it is necessary to abandon ourselves completely to Him, allowing Him to work in all His fullness. When we get to that point, we no longer assert our own will over His will; rather, we freely surrender to His purposes and desires.

As we die to ourselves, we become one with God. That is why the apostle Paul declared:

I have been crucified with Christ; it is no longer I who live, but Christ lives in me; and the life which I now live in the flesh I live by faith in the Son of God, who loved me and gave Himself for me. I do not set aside the grace of God; for if righteousness comes through the law, then Christ died in vain. (Galatians 2:20–21)

> ## The flow of the supernatural begins when we know the will of God and remain in it.

Thus, to know God's will, we must surrender completely to Him, just as Christ gave Himself completely to the Father. One of the keys to the success of Jesus's life was that He continually stayed in God's will. His obedience was a natural part of His life, because He was always one with the Father. As the Son of God, He knew that no one can move in the supernatural without being one with the Father; He also knew that there can be no manifestations of power apart from the will of God. Furthermore, the more we know God, the more we know ourselves. If we know our identity in Him, as Jesus knew His, and if we remain in His will, as Jesus did, then we will receive power and authority to act on God's behalf.

We know that Jesus came to restore the unity between God and man, so we could have intimacy with the Father and become one with Him again. Being one with God comes as a result of being aligned with His will. And being one with God means that, when we speak, we come into agreement with the Father to do His will on earth.

Do you know the will of God for your personal life? Do you know His will for your ministry or your career? Do you know who you are in God, and what you should do on His behalf? The mystery is that we are being empowered through our union with Him. There is power in communion and relationship with the God of heaven, because it is in that fellowship that He shares His image and glory with us. There, we can see His face and see ourselves in Him, as in a mirror. There, we come to know Him and understand His eternal will.

> When we remain in the will of God,
> we are empowered.

3. Do the Will of God

"But be doers of the word, and not hearers only, deceiving yourselves" (James 1:22). It is not enough to know the will of God; it is necessary to *do* it. If we don't act on it, we will become merely "religious" and our faith will fade, no matter how much knowledge we have. When we do His will, we are synchronized with the rhythm of faith. *"Faith comes by hearing, and hearing by the word of God"* (Romans 10:17)—but we see the manifestation of our faith by acting on what we have heard from God. Not doing God's will is the same as never having heard it. When someone doesn't act according to the spiritual knowledge they have received or learned, the devil comes and makes them doubt, and the rhythm of faith is lost. (See, for example, Matthew 13:19.)

> Jesus's greatest motivation was to do
> the will of His Father.

Jesus persevered in doing the will of the Father; in fact, the Father's will was His daily food, as He Himself said: *"My food is to do the will of Him who sent Me, and to finish His work"* (John 4:34). Many times, the enemy tried to kill the Son of God, but he was unable to. We must remember that Jesus died on the cross only at the direction of the

Father, and only in the fullness of time. He laid down His own life for the Father's purposes of saving the world through Him. (See John 10:17–18.) Remaining in the Father's will is therefore equivalent to being surrounded by the best shield of protection one could imagine. That is why Jesus always had peace, even amid persecution.

> We don't remain in the will of God by accident, but by intentional obedience to the revelation of His purposes.

4. Speak According to the Will of God

The fourth fundamental principle for having our prayers answered is that we must speak the will of God. This refers to declaring and decreeing His will, which is the same as giving spiritual commands. If we know God, His will has been revealed to us, and if we remain in His will and act on it, then when we speak, His answer will be immediate.

Many times, a sick person has approached me, and the only thing I do to bring healing is to declare that they are healed in the name of Jesus. God works in them instantly! This happens because I have spent time in the presence of God, and His will to heal people has been revealed to me. I try to know, remain in, and do the will of the Father at all times so that the moment I declare something, His supernatural power can flow without hindrance. I learned this from Jesus, because when He performed miracles, He didn't pray and ask God to heal the sick; instead, He declared, "Be healed!" or "Rise up and walk!" When we are living in unity with God's will and we declare something, it is as if God Himself is speaking, because we decree on His behalf, with His authority and from His identity.

When we are aligned with the will of God,
we don't speak in order for something to happen,
but because we know it has already happened
in the spiritual realm.

Consequently, if your life is aligned with the above four principles of God's will, you are synchronized with the supernatural and you have access to the power and authority of God. You now have the same power that Jesus had when He was on earth, in order to act in His name. Jesus said, *"I can of Myself do nothing. As I hear, I judge; and My judgment is righteous, because I do not seek My own will but the will of the Father who sent Me"* (John 5:30). Again, this knowledge of the Father's will was the secret of His success when He had to demonstrate the power of God.

Jesus is the only way to the Father (see John 14:6), and He is our role model. If Jesus knew the will of God, then you, too, must know it. If Jesus was in the will of God, then you, too, must be in His will. If Jesus's actions were led by the will of God, then your actions must also be led by that will. If Jesus spoke according to the will of God, then you must do the same. Then there won't be any obstacles to receiving answers to your prayers. There will be a complete flow of the supernatural that will bring the fulfillment of the Father's will in each situation.

Let me ask you again: Do you know the will of God for your personal life, your marriage, and your finances? Are you in the will of God? Are you doing the will of God? Are you praying according to the will of God? Whoever is aligned with the will of God prays and receives answers from Him. Today is the day that your prayer life goes to another dimension; it accelerates and moves *"from faith to faith"* (Romans 1:17) and from answer to answer! Don't accept delays anymore. Acceleration can come because what you declare is God's eternal will, which transcends the linear passage of time. If there are still unanswered prayers, it is because you have not applied one of the four principles, or have not fully aligned yourself with the will of God in relation to one or more of them.

Aligning with the four principles of God's will for receiving answers to prayer will remove stagnation, barriers, and strongholds—and will bring acceleration.

The Rhythm of the Supernatural

You enter into the rhythm of the supernatural when you are aligned with the work of God in the now—with what God is doing today. That is where acceleration comes. There are answers to prayer being held back because the prayers are not aligned with heaven—line up your life with God's will! There are barriers that are impeding your answer from coming—yet these are broken now, in the name of Jesus! The rhythm of the supernatural is released now! This is the same rhythm in which Jesus operated as a Man, as He lived according to the four principles of God's will. Once again, when He stood in front of the tomb of Lazarus, about to speak the word of resurrection, *"Jesus lifted up His eyes and said, 'Father, I thank You that You have heard Me. And I know that You always hear Me, but because of the people who are standing by I said this, that they may believe that You sent Me'"* (John 11:41–42).

Beloved reader, more than inviting you to do so, I want to challenge you to start making declarations according to the will of God. Declare and decree your healing, your deliverance, and your transformation. Don't pray, "Father, if it is Your will...," because Jesus has already established His will for you. It is done; it is already finished. Now is the time for breakthrough!

> When you are aligned with the will of God, faith is now.

Activation

It is necessary to examine our hearts to make sure we have truly aligned ourselves with the will of God. If we haven't been speaking and acting according to His perfect will, we are in sin due to disobedience; therefore, we must repent and line ourselves up with His purposes and desires. The moment we repent, we will be in harmony with heaven, and then acceleration will come to every area of our lives.

If you really want to be in agreement with God's will, I invite you to say the following prayer:

Beloved heavenly Father, I come before Your presence affirming You as the almighty God, the Lord of the universe, and the Lord of my life. You are God, and there is no true life outside of You. I know You hear my prayer because I am in Your presence and the Holy Spirit guides my intercession. I repent and ask You to forgive me for ignoring Your will in my prayers. Starting today, I make a commitment to know Your will, to be—and to remain in—Your will, to do Your will, and to speak Your will.

I pray from heaven to earth, which is the position that Christ won for us through His work at the cross. My faith is now, and all that You have spoken in heaven, I speak on earth, declaring that Your promises and mighty works come into existence in my life, in my family, in my ministry, in my nation, in Your church, and in all Your children. I speak Your will for Your kingdom to come on earth as it is in heaven. I declare there is healing for the sick! I declare there is prosperity for the poor! I declare there is protection and refuge for the widow and the orphan! I declare there is supernatural grace for Your children to attain Your promises, expand Your kingdom, and preach Your gospel throughout the world! I thank You for the revelation of the four principles for having our prayers answered, according to Your perfect will. I thank You for the breakthrough You bring to my life with this revelation. I pray all this in the name that is above all names—the name of Jesus. Amen!

Testimonies of Breakthrough Prayer

Supernaturally Prospered

The following testimony from Wilmer demonstrates what it means to pray according to the will of God:

> Thanks to God, King Jesus Ministry has taught me a pattern that has led me to success. Last year, I got together with my family to pray and plan what amount our firstfruits offering to God would be this year. I wanted to give an unusual offering, more than we normally give, expecting an unusual breakthrough, but I wanted it to be in alignment with God's will. Accordingly, we gave our firstfruits, but after a few months, nothing unusual happened. January, February, March, and April passed...yet there was nothing. The month of August came, and I was frustrated, so I started to claim my breakthrough. Then I realized that I was failing God—my faith had weakened, and I had stopped praying; I had neglected my time of intimacy with Him. I immediately began to pray. A few minutes later, a man called and offered me a job. I appropriated that as the answer from God, and I presented it to Him, believing the project would come through. I went to the man's place of business, and I left with a contract for $110,000!
>
> But that's not the testimony. Two weeks later, after Hurricane Irma had passed through Miami, I went to get gas for my car, but since all the gas stations nearby were full, I drove around the streets looking for another gas station, until I found one that was available. Once there, I felt the Holy Spirit leading me to

speak specifically to one man. I approached him and spoke to him about Christ; as we kept talking, he told me he owned that service station and was looking for someone to repair the lights. I told him that's what I do, and right there we signed a contract. What I didn't know was that this man owned two hundred gas stations, and the total contract was for $1.2 million!

Healed from Terminal Osteoporosis

I recently traveled to Ethiopia in Africa for the second time, sent by God to hold a Supernatural Encounter, bring the message of the gospel of the kingdom, and manifest His power. Among the numerous testimonies from this time, I would like to share the following:

My name is Tigist, and I'm from Addis Ababa. For three years, I had a severe form of osteoporosis. I was quickly losing bone mass and mobility. The doctors had declared me terminally ill and had sent me home, with no hope of getting better. Bedridden, I couldn't urinate sitting down, I couldn't feed myself, and I couldn't even sit or sleep normally. My two children took care of me, but while they were in school, I stayed home alone, and I used to wait in a fetal position until they came home to help me. I cried to God and begged Him to have mercy on me. I cried so much that my eyes were always irritated. My only hope was God!

One day, some people invited me to a conference where they said God's supernatural power would move to heal the sick. When the day came, they placed me on a blanket and took me there in a taxi. I arrived at the place with five broken bones in my back; it was impossible for me to walk. Apostle Maldonado was preaching about the power of the cross, saying that healing belongs to all the children of God, that His will is to heal us. Then, he started declaring that according to the will of God, those who were paralyzed would be healed in the name of Jesus; they only had to rise and walk. That instant, I felt a strong heat on my back and I started moving. Seconds later, I was standing up! I had stood up on my own. Then I started walking; I left behind the cane I had used to support myself, and I could walk without any limitation! Everyone was amazed! When I returned home, everyone there also looked at me amazed; they couldn't understand what had happened. My children and neighbors were so happy to see me healthy again.

From that moment, I started telling everyone that Jesus had healed me, and that His will is to heal everyone, because that is why He paid the penalty on the cross. I am not ashamed of this message, and I don't care if people reject me or don't want to hear me. I know what Jesus did in my body. He did what no one else had been able to do. For God, nothing is impossible! He gave me a new life!

Freed from Deep Depression

My name is Gabriela, and I can say that before coming to the feet of Christ, I didn't have a life. I breathed, but spiritually I was dead. I wasn't the mother my children needed me to be; they were essentially alone. My husband had left me, and that had been a trigger for depression to completely take hold of my emotions. I was eventually hospitalized in a psychiatric clinic, where the doctors said I would never recover. I was released from the clinic, but I was stuck. I was a pharmacist, and the depression was so deep that I lived only to work. Yet my finances were going from bad to worse. I spent a lot of money buying pills illegally—because the thirty pills that had been prescribed to last a month, I had taken in only two days.

I looked for help in many places, but could find none. One night, I tried to commit suicide with pills, and I was hospitalized due to the overdose. At that point, I no longer saw a way out for my life. I decided I wanted my children to go live with their grandparents because I didn't have anything to offer them. Their life by my side was a disaster.

One day, I woke up in another hospital where they wouldn't let me out at first; but when I pretended to be better, they discharged me. Even so, my problems were still there, and my four children and I continued to live in a rented room. I was unable to work in my profession or advance in anything. I told myself, *I need a change; I'm going to that church, King Jesus, where they say that miracles happen.*

As soon as I arrived at the church, I threw myself in front of the altar and told God, "If you are the Lord they speak about here, I know that You are going to do it." I left the church at three in the afternoon, and I slept from the moment I came home until the next day at eight in the morning, without taking any pills. From that day, I felt different. I still didn't know it, but that Sunday I went home with my miracle. When I returned for the next service, I knelt in the same place and said, "Lord, thank You for saving my life. From now on, my children and I will serve You with all our hearts."

Ever since I went to the church, my life has changed completely. I can practice my profession; in fact, I've had a stable job for seven months now. I went from not having a home or a car to having both; each one of my children now has their own bedroom and lives like every child should live. Best of all, the five of us are committed to God. We win souls for Christ with the testimony of what we went through. I had a very bad time, but my children had it worse than I did. I am thankful because, before, I didn't believe I deserved the joy of Christ; I didn't even know what joy was. Now, I know that His will is for us to be happy. I know where Christ rescued me from. He took me out of the darkest and deepest place a person can ever be. Thank You, Lord!

7

PRAYING WITH THE WORD OF GOD

"I am ready to perform My word."
—Jeremiah 1:12

In the book of Genesis, we read that the serpent (Satan), the most cunning of all the animals in the field, went to the garden of Eden to sow doubts about God in the minds of Adam and Eve, and to tempt them to disobey Him. With that plan, he approached the woman and said to her, *"Has God indeed said…?"* (Genesis 3:1). Eve knew the instructions God had given to the man for them to follow (see Genesis 2:16–17), but she didn't answer the serpent in accordance with those instructions; this is how the curse entered the world and Adam and Eve lost their fellowship with the Father. Thousands of years later, Satan wanted to use the same tactic with Jesus, but when he went to tempt the Son of God in the desert, Jesus answered, *"It is written, 'Man shall not live by bread alone, but by every word that proceeds from the mouth of God'"* (Matthew 4:4). With this response, God's plan for the redemption of humanity began to unfold.

In our day, God requires His people to return to His Word. His Word alone justifies and endorses the petitions and declarations we make in prayer before His throne. Jesus taught His disciples, *"And whatever you ask in My name, that I will do, that the Father may be glorified in the Son"* (John 14:13). In the original Greek, the word translated *"ask"* here means, among other things, to require, wish, or demand something. This means that when we go before God supported by His Word, we can put in a claim, or a "demand," for what He has said. We must understand that when we do this, we are not giving orders to God! Rather, it is a declaration of faith, knowing that what He promises in His Word is fulfilled in the now.

In other words, you must be willing to say, for example, "Lord, Your Word says that by Your stripes I am healed, so I am placing a demand on my healing," or "Lord, Your Word says You will supply all my needs according to Your riches in glory by Christ Jesus, so I put a claim on Your provision for my life." (See Isaiah 53:5; 1 Peter 2:24; Philippians 4:19.) When you pray in this way, you make God responsible for your petition. The prophet Hosea said, *"Take words with you, and return to the LORD. Say to Him, 'Take away all iniquity; receive us graciously, for we will offer the sacrifices of our lips'"* (Hosea 14:2). Thus, if you are maintaining an intimate relationship with God, if you are standing in a position of righteousness and walking in His will, if you begin your prayers by affirming the greatness of the Lord, and if your request is aligned with His Word, then He will honor and fulfill your petition.

When God's Word is the substance of our prayers, and we are in right relationship with Him, it commits Him to give us an answer.

"Soulish" Prayers Versus Word Prayers

Praying from the soul, or from the center of our desires and emotions, is not the same as praying from the Word. The former is known as a "soulish" prayer. Our souls are not always aligned with God's purposes, so when people pray in this way, they often ask God for things He has not promised to give, or they declare things that are not in His Word. These prayers are usually based in self-pity, and they are attempts to control or manipulate a situation. Additionally, they are subjective because, depending on the emotion of the moment, a person might ask for one thing or the other. What they ask for has no stability to it, much less any divine foundation or kingdom purpose. And of course, such prayers cannot guarantee a miracle. The worst part is, prayers that come purely from our emotions—those that, in effect, try to manipulate God to give us something—stem from the spirit of witchcraft, because in witchcraft, one seeks to control people and situations to one's own advantage.

What should we do in order to pray correctly? We must stop praying from the center of our emotions and start praying according to the solid foundation of God's Word. Let's keep in mind that our emotions change depending on the temporary circumstances in our lives, but the Word of God is constant; it doesn't change or contradict itself. When we go to God in prayer, we must declare, "Lord, Your Word says _____, and this is what I need to happen in my life."

Every prayer we make based on the Word must appeal to and affirm the victory of the cross.

Our Knowledge of the Word

Most Christians begin their walk with Christ discipled by mentors, spiritual fathers and mothers, or others who have preceded them in the faith; as these new believers grow spiritually, they depend on the prayers of others. This is fine, because that is what Christ and the apostles taught us to do in the discipleship process. But we are also instructed that we need to mature in our faith. That means we must learn to pray for ourselves, so we no longer have to depend on another's prayers for our growth and steadfastness in the faith. Of course, we all benefit from one another's prayers. Yet we must learn for ourselves what to pray and how to pray.

When Jesus was on earth, He relied on His own prayer life, on His knowledge of God's Word, and on the revelation of the Holy Spirit. This is the will of the Father for all His children—and it should be the goal of every Christian to do the same. God is asking that we return to Him by offering prayers based on His own Word, and He is testing the church to see how strong and continuous our prayer life is.

Knowledge is always a powerful "currency" or "good of exchange," and our ability to influence our situations and the world around us will increase as our knowledge of God's Word increases. We will never rise or grow beyond our level of knowledge; therefore, we must continually seek to increase our knowledge of God and His Word, for the purpose of being established in the truth. *"For this reason I will not be negligent to remind you always of these things, though you know and are established in the present truth"* (2 Peter 1:12).

Our knowledge of the Word increases our spiritual treasure and our capacity to influence the world as we walk in the supernatural.

Qualities of the Word

As we pray with God's Word, we must recognize and apply these qualities connected with it:

The Word of God Is His Will

The Word of God is the direct expression of His will, and nothing or no one can change it. Neither disease, nor poverty, nor any other adverse circumstance can alter its truth. If you want to know the will of God, the most appropriate place to begin is with His Word. One of the main reasons the Holy Spirit inspired the writing of the books that comprise the Bible is to make God known to us, and to communicate His mind and will to us.

> When we pray with the Word, we are praying the will of God.

The Word of God Endures

"But the word of the LORD endures forever.' Now this is the word which by the gospel was preached to you" (1 Peter 1:25). The word *"endures"* indicates that something exists continuously; it never ceases to be. When we go before God, we must remain in Him and hold on to what His eternal Word says—even in the middle of the worst situation we may be going through.

The Word of God Transcends Time, Space, and Matter

The Word of God always goes forth to answer a need, regardless of the place or how far away those who require the help may be. When we speak the Word, if those needing help are in another city or another country, the Word will manifest in that place, because it doesn't travel according to the laws of time, space, and matter, but rather in the now, in the eternal. *"So shall My word be that goes forth from My mouth; it shall not return to Me void, but it shall accomplish what I please, and it shall prosper in the thing for which I sent it"* (Isaiah 55:11).

There is no earthly or demonic power that can say no to the Word of God. There is no wall that can stop it, or distance that can delay it. Again, there is no sickness, disease, depression, or poverty that can thwart its fulfillment. Nothing stops it! Every sick person is healed, every oppressed person is delivered, and all poverty is eradicated. The provision of God comes at any time and at any place. The only requirement is that the Word of God be declared according to the will of God and in the name of Jesus. At the same moment the Word is declared, it is activated and comes into existence in the natural world.

The Word of God Contains the Power of God

Let us look at two points in relation to this quality of God's Word:

1. *The power of God resides in His Word, and then it acts in us.* In other words, the power is not in us, but in the Word of God, from where any anointed person may take it. Ephesians 3:20 says, *"Now to Him who is able to do exceedingly abundantly above all that we ask or think, according to the power that works in us."*

Before working in a person, the supernatural power of God resides in His Word.

When we understand where the power of God resides, it changes our way of thinking and of declaring the Word. I want to reiterate this, because if you understand this principle well, you will know that every believer can be used to manifest the power of God. I repeat, the power is not in a person, but in the Word of God. That is why the apostle Peter said, *"If anyone speaks, let him speak as the oracles of God. If anyone ministers, let him do it as with the ability which God supplies, that in all things God may be glorified through Jesus Christ"* (1 Peter 4:11).

2. *The power of God resides in His mouth, because that is from where His Word proceeds.* Jesus said, *"It is written, 'Man shall not live by bread alone, but by every word that proceeds from the mouth of God'"* (Matthew 4:4). When you speak the Word with authority, you can declare that mountains move, doors open, your body is healed, your mind is free, and salvation comes to your family, because you are God's spokesperson on earth!

When we are in the presence of God, we can make a declaration, according to His Word, against anything the enemy has used as a weapon to destroy someone's life. Thus, when you are before Him, proclaim what the Scripture says, because God is one with His Word. As noted earlier, this means He is obligated to fulfill what He has already said. Seek God and take His Word wherever you go. Speak the Word and send it to the nations to heal, deliver, and do the will of God!

Don't forget that any prayer that is not based on the Word is a soulish prayer. It is usually centered only on the needs of the person who is praying and is founded on self-pity and a desire to control. Generally, God doesn't answer that kind of prayer, because nothing from Him is in those words, and He is not obliged to answer it. God wants you to declare His Word. He will always respond to what He has already said, but it hasn't yet all been fulfilled on earth.

The Word of God Doesn't Have an Expiration Date

Jesus left us this promise: *"Heaven and earth will pass away, but My words will by no means pass away"* (Matthew 24:35). This means that, if your circumstances are not aligned with the Word of God, but you put a claim on them according to that Word, they will have to change, because the Word doesn't change. If the Word would ever pass away, then the sun, the moon, the stars, the light, and everything else would also pass away! Nothing, whether visible or invisible, would exist, because Christ is *"upholding all things by the word of His power"* (Hebrews 1:3).

Therefore, even if people tell you it's too late to receive a miracle, know that God's Word doesn't have an expiration date. And God is never late! Tell your problem what God has already established in eternity. The doctor may give you a negative diagnosis, but the Word says that *"by [Jesus's] stripes we are healed"* (Isaiah 53:5). Which report will you believe? Will you believe the medical report or the Word of God? The Scriptures say that Christ became poor for our sakes so that we might prosper. (See 2 Corinthians 8:9.) Will you believe the negative balance in your bank account, or will you believe what the Word says? How credible is the Word of God to you? Let me tell you that the Word is everlasting and infinite. It is as valid today as it was yesterday—and as it will be tomorrow. That is why we shouldn't go to God with our human opinions, ideas, or experiences, but only with His Word. God is greater than our opinions, ideas, and past experiences. *"Then the LORD said to me, 'You have seen well, for I am ready to perform My word'"* (Jeremiah 1:12). Let Him perform His Word!

Activation

Dear reader, if you have been praying according to human ideas and wisdom, rather than according to the Word of God, I invite you to pray the following prayer out loud:

Beloved heavenly Father, I thank You for the revelation I am receiving through these pages. I repent for having said prayers that were born from my opinions, ideas, and experiences and not from Your Word. I recognize that many of my petitions haven't been answered because they weren't aligned with Your will. Today, with the help of the Holy Spirit, I make the decision to read the Bible more so I can better understand Your will and pray accordingly. I also commit to seeking You in prayer in order to know Your *rhema* word—the word You have today for my life, my family, my work, and my ministry. I will pray according to Your eternal Word, which never expires, which sustains itself, which directs me into Your will, which transcends time, space, and matter, and which goes forth from Your mouth full of power. Starting now, my prayers will no longer be empty, because You have said, *"So shall My word be that goes forth from My mouth; it shall not return to Me void, but it shall accomplish what I please, and it shall prosper in the thing for which I sent it."* In Jesus's name, amen! (See Isaiah 55:11.)

Testimonies of Breakthrough Prayer

A Baby Girl Healed of Down Syndrome

Diana Finkelstein is a prophet in our ministry. She passed along this testimony of a young couple who were told their baby girl would be born with Down Syndrome, until God intervened and radically changed the medical prognosis.

Paul and Nicole are a young couple from our church in Miami. They love the Lord and serve Him with all their hearts. The only thing they were missing was a child. In fact, they had been married for more than five years without being able to conceive, which didn't make sense since both of them are healthy. While I was praying for them, the Holy Spirit gave me a word and led me to pray for that specific situation. Finally, after years of waiting, God intervened and Nicole became pregnant.

However, one day, Nicole came looking for me because, in a routine exam, the doctor told her that their baby would be born with Down Syndrome. Immediately, I knew that was a lie from the enemy, and I told them that if they believed and accepted that diagnosis, their baby would be born like that, but if they chose to believe what the Word of God says, they would see His power manifested. Of course, they chose to believe God, so I prayed and gave them instructions to confess Psalm 139 with faith. They believed and were obedient. When they went to their next appointment with the doctor, they told her they didn't receive the Down Syndrome diagnosis, and they wanted her to repeat the test. Even though the doctor became upset, the new test results showed that the baby was completely healthy! And that's how she was born—healthy. Today, she is a beautiful three-year-old who is her parents' joy.

These young parents declared the Word of God, prayed according to His perfect will, and received this powerful miracle. Glory to God!

Supernatural Wisdom for an HIV Cure

My name is Teka, and I live in Addis Ababa, the capital of Ethiopia. I am a firm believer in Christ and a missionary in my country. Last year, I went to the Supernatural Encounter conference that took place in Ethiopia, where Apostle Maldonado preached to pastors and leaders. While Apostle was ministering the infilling of the Holy Spirit, he approached me and said, "God is going to impart wisdom in you, and He is going to activate you to do unusual things." I received that word with faith, but I never imagined what was coming: God gave me wisdom to develop a cure for HIV.

For ten years, I had suffered from that disease, but I had kept it a secret. However, I never went through any antiretroviral therapy; I just took good care of myself and prayed for a divine intervention, looking for the way to receive healing. After that impartation from Apostle Maldonado, God gave me the wisdom to discover the necessary ingredients to develop an herbal medicine that reverts the traces of the virus in the blood. I researched and tested the effectiveness of the product on myself. After a process of trial and error, I took a blood test, and the result came out negative for HIV. Since this was remarkable, I went to another clinic to have the test done once more, and the result was again HIV-negative. I repeated the test in a third clinic, and the result was the same—negative!

After having the test done five times, I made an appointment with the government to patent the medicine I had developed and file the necessary paperwork with the agency that regulates medicines, and then I registered it. I have given it free to some volunteers, and the news has begun to spread. My plan is to help virus carriers who, after being diagnosed, don't have any other medical options. As of today, fifty-one people, including myself, have ceased to carry this virus, for which we give glory and honor to our God. I am so thankful to Him for using me to help them all. Jesus said, *"If you can believe, all things are possible to him who believes"* (Mark 9:23). I believed, and what was impossible became a reality! I praise God, and I will use this supernatural wisdom to magnify and exalt His name all around the world. Jesus is our Lord and our Healer!

A Baby Resurrected from the Dead

Rory, who lives in Johannesburg, the largest city in South Africa, has a powerful testimony of what it means to declare the Word of God.

Some time ago, I received a desperate call from my daughter; she was screaming that she had found her son floating in her home's backyard pool. The child was only a year and a half, and he had drowned. He was rushed to the hospital and connected to a machine to keep him alive. The doctors said they couldn't do anything else for him and that he had to be disconnected, but my daughter told them, "If there isn't anything else you can do, I put my son in Jesus's hands." A few hours later, the report we received was that he had died due to the amount of water in his lungs. I didn't know what to say to my daughter; I took a deep breath and asked the Holy Spirit to help me. Suddenly, I remembered I had received an impartation about this. I had been in a leadership meeting with Apostle Maldonado in which he had taught us that we have authority to declare the power of Christ's resurrection over the dead. At that time, many people from our daughter churches had gathered in the church to have a prayer vigil for my grandson.

The next day, I traveled to the hospital to see my family. Everyone was devastated, and even though I have great faith, in that moment, I could barely breathe. I looked at my grandson—still on artificial life support—all covered with tubes and lifeless. I took some oil and started anointing his body. Then I prayed, saying, "Lord, I believe in You. I believe You raised Lazarus from the dead. I didn't see it, but I know that same power is with me here today. I want that supernatural power to touch my grandson." As I was praying, the baby suddenly started squirming. Life was coming back into him! The nurses came running because the machine alarms had started to sound. His lungs had recovered! My grandson had resurrected, for the glory of God!

8

KEYS TO BREAKTHROUGH PRAYER

"Sow for yourselves righteousness; reap in mercy; break up your fallow ground, for it is time to seek the Lord, till He comes and rains righteousness on you."
—Hosea 10:12

A lack of consistency is very evident in the church at this time. We see people rushing to attend isolated ministry events instead of pursuing a continuous and growing infilling of the Holy Spirit. The apostle Paul wrote, *"Be filled with the Spirit"* (Ephesians 5:18), but the church has largely chosen to ignore this mandate, not realizing that, as long as we fail to acknowledge it, the breakthroughs we're waiting for will not come. We are part of a generation that knows a lot about doctrines and Christian traditions but does not know the principles of the kingdom of God, knows about natural laws but very little about spiritual laws, and knows how to fight for their rights as citizens of earthly nations but has not been able to appropriate the heavenly, spiritual rights that Jesus has already won for us on the cross.

God always works through principles and patterns. The Scriptures show us that prayer is a practice that requires consistency and continuity, and that prayer is one of the main patterns of spiritual growth. "Praying without ceasing" (see 1 Thessalonians 5:17) leads us to overcome every challenge that life presents us and every obstacle that the enemy raises to try to stop our advancement in Christ. Thus, if you cease praying about your situation, you will not see a breakthrough, and you won't find out that you may have been only one or two steps away from receiving your miracle or blessing, because you gave up before your breakthrough came. The enemy's plan will always be directed at making you quit before receiving the answer to your prayer.

The Need for Breakthrough

Satan is desperate to thwart the work of God, and he will try to hinder believers by any means possible. When we come against his attacks, we need breakthroughs in prayer—allowing us to live above demonic interferences (as well as natural obstacles), from miracle to miracle! However, achieving a breakthrough is not a matter of simply pressing a button. Our prayers must be continuous and persistent—until a miracle takes place, provision comes, sickness leaves the body, children return home, or whatever else we are believing for happens.

When continuity in prayer stops, momentum in the Spirit is halted.

The devil wants to interrupt the rhythm of the supernatural in us. When he achieves it, it is as if he has constructed a huge wall blocking the path that connects us to God's blessings. When we lose contact with the supernatural, we begin to slow down and lose momentum in the Spirit. In cases like that, we urgently need a breakthrough!

How do we achieve this breakthrough? By praising God until His power falls and by worshipping Him until His presence comes! When the Israelites were slaves in Egypt, they cried out for four hundred and thirty years to be delivered from their captivity. Then, God called Moses to bring them out of Egypt and lead them to the promised land. In the process, they had to go through the desert, cross the Red Sea, and overcome many rebellions in their ranks. Moses carried the momentum for breakthrough in himself; but, to serve the purposes of God, he had first needed forty years of experience in Pharaoh's palace, living according to a freedom mentality, and then forty more years of tough training in the desert as a shepherd. Finally, in the fullness of time, the sum of all this preparation turned him into the answer from God to the accumulated prayers of a whole group of people.

> For a breakthrough to come upon a people or a nation, prayer accumulation is needed.

The enemy's plan has always been to steal, kill, and destroy (see John 10:10); that is why, when he sends an attack against our life, we need a swift breakthrough. There may be occasions when you feel hindered or limited in your circumstances to such an extent that you seem to be paralyzed; this is because the enemy has you in chains. Moreover, you can tell when a demonic restriction is touching your life as a whole because you feel the need of multiple breakthroughs. In reality, most of us need breakthroughs in various areas of our lives— for example, in our personal life, our family, our business, our education, our health, and even in our emotions. Breakthroughs must include deliverance, because demonic bonds are preventing us from moving forward in supernatural power, from knowing more about God, from leaving behind a sinful life, or from persevering in prayer.

What Is Breakthrough Prayer?

To break is defined as "to separate into parts with suddenness or violence." Similarly, breakthrough prayer generates an abrupt, violent, and sudden rupture of what is hindering us, pushing us beyond that limitation and into freedom. Breakthrough prayer must be engaged in persistently and consistently until we sense that something has broken in the spiritual realm, and until what we are asking for manifests. With a breakthrough, what we need is brought from the spiritual world to the natural world, so that we can see it in a visible or tangible demonstration of God's power or provision.

Therefore, breakthrough prayer requires the ability to persevere and endure, to keep pressing on and resisting with courage. It necessitates relentless diligence, tenacity, boldness, and importunity—the capacity to stand firmly against opposition until you see the answer. We must develop a faith characterized by holy stubbornness and daring, unafraid to challenge what comes against us.

For breakthrough prayer, we must also maintain an outlook that sees beyond what is naturally impossible to what is supernaturally possible. We see an example of this in the encounter between Naaman and the prophet Elisha. (See 2 Kings 5:1–14.) Naaman was a general in the Syrian army who was great and courageous before his king—but he suffered from leprosy. When Naaman went to Elisha for help, and the prophet ordered him to dip seven times in the Jordan river, he first thought that it made no sense; in fact, he became angry and was about to leave before he was persuaded by his servant to follow the prophet's instructions.

What would have happened if Naaman had left without obeying? What would have happened if he had dipped only once? What if he had stopped at the sixth time? He would not have been healed. However, his willingness to persist in full obedience led him to obtain his miracle.

Maybe you are experiencing something similar. Perhaps you are a brave and important man or woman, but you are suffering from a condition that, in your own strength, is impossible to remedy. This story about Naaman illustrates specific keys to breakthrough prayer, which we will explore next.

Spiritual Keys to Breakthrough Prayer

1. Breakthrough Prayer Is Continuous, Consistent, Persistent, and Perseverant

Sow for yourselves righteousness; reap in mercy; break up your fallow ground, for it is time to seek the LORD, till He comes and rains righteousness on you. (Hosea 10:12)

The exercise of perseverance has the same effect in the spiritual realm that it does in the natural. For example, in the physical world, if you want to lose weight, you must persevere and be consistent by maintaining the appropriate diet and engaging in regular exercise. Or, if you want to obtain a university degree, you must continue until you complete your study program. There are some people who start out with great enthusiasm and obtain early results; for example, they drop ten pounds (about five kilograms) of the thirty they want to lose; or they progress successfully through two years of studies in a four-year program—but then, when their progress slows or things get a bit more difficult, they become discouraged and quit. Doubt and inconsistency have derailed their purposes. The Bible says that *"a double-minded man* [is] *unstable in all his ways*" (James 1:8). Such a person will never finish anything!

God wants us to conquer various spiritual territories—in our lives, in others' lives, and in the world—that are currently being held by the enemy and can only be recovered for His kingdom by continuous prayers of faith. Jesus Himself needed to pray constantly and persistently in order to conquer the territories the Father had assigned to Him. His mission was to displace Satan and establish the kingdom of God on earth. It was not an easy task because, due to the sin of the first human beings, the devil had legal authority on the earth. Jesus knew that only in prayer would He be able to overcome; that is why He won the battle of the cross as He prayed in the garden of Gethsemane the night before He was crucified. Once more, we can see that the church needs to recover the spirit of prayer with which it was born. If there is no demand in prayer, we will not be able to obtain the necessary mega-breakthroughs in these end times.

> Anything you want to achieve in God requires that you not give up, but persevere until it happens.

2. Spiritual Breakthrough Doesn't Happen by Chance

There are some acts that God does sovereignly, but there are others we must participate in if they are to happen. One of the biggest deceptions people can fall into is to believe that the manifestations of the Spirit, like miracles, signs, wonders, or God's supernatural provision, occur "just because." For example, a Christian leader might, one time, enter the realm of the supernatural because they happen to follow a spiritual principle without realizing it. However, since they don't have sufficient knowledge of who God is, how the supernatural operates, or the laws of the spiritual realm such as breakthrough prayer, they can't advance in supernatural power. Consequently, they end up believing and teaching that God merely "acts in mysterious ways" that can't be anticipated. Others might walk in the supernatural "by association" because they are close to a man or woman of God who knows the spiritual principles and moves in the supernatural. However, unless they receive a personal revelation of why miracles and breakthroughs occur, they won't be able to operate in the supernatural themselves.

> You will not be able to continue operating in a spiritual reality you discover by accident, because you will not understand how it came to you.

As noted above, God always works through principles and patterns, not by chance. We can see that there was a pattern to everything that Jesus did. As a Man, He knew the principles and laws for moving in the supernatural. There was always a kingdom principle behind each one of His words and acts, which were based on revelation from the Father. Nothing He did happened by accident. We see an example of this when it came time for Him to make the weighty decision of choosing His twelve closest disciples. *"It came to pass in those days that He went out to the mountain to pray, and continued all night in prayer to God. And when it was day, He called His disciples to Himself; and from them He chose twelve whom He also named apostles"* (Luke 6:12–13).

It is clear that Jesus never did anything in a casual way. In this case, He knew He had to choose disciples who could be sent out as apostles, and that is why He spent the whole night beforehand praying. Let me ask you, does God need a whole night to do something? Of course not! When God does something in His sovereignty, time is not a factor. God is above time, space, and matter. However, human beings operate within the framework of time and the limitations of a finite mind, so it takes us longer. You may be thinking, *But if Jesus is God, why did He have to pray all night long? Didn't He transcend time, too? Didn't He have an infinite mind?* The answer is that Jesus, as the Son of God, didn't operate as God on the earth, but as a Man, so He could be mankind's full representative in His life and in His death. In order to transcend time and finite thinking and enter the eternal realm, He needed to commune with the Father in prayer.

> Praying all night produces mega-anointing, and this releases mega-miracles.

Jesus's prayer life was the key to all the healings and deliverances from demonic oppression that He ministered to people. The price that He paid while praying at night bore fruit in His ministry during the day. His continuous prayer life generated so much power in His spirit that, every time He went anywhere, the demons fled in terror. *"Those who were tormented with unclean spirits…were healed. And the whole multitude sought to touch Him, for power went out from Him and healed them all"* (Luke 6:18–19).

Jesus revolutionized the towns and cities He visited because, before He went, He was filled with power in prayer. He bound the demonic strong man (see Mark 3:27) that governed over those regions and conquered those territories. In other words, during the night, Jesus gave commands regarding what would happen during the next day. He saw ahead in the Spirit and declared what was going to occur, according to the will of the Father. Prayer is also how He built up His spirit for what the next day would bring.

Jesus passed this pattern of continual prayer along to His disciples, and they followed it; in turn, they instructed the believers in the early church, who lived according to the same pattern of prayer. We must do likewise; if we don't, someone else will determine what will occur during our day and dictate the outcome, and we won't be able to prevent it. I believe this is the time in the history of the church when God wants to manifest mega-miracles, mega-provision, and mega-blessings, but none of these things will happen "just because"; they will require continuous, consistent, and persistent prayer.

> Miracles, signs, and wonders do not happen very often nowadays because there is little demand for them in prayer.

Having a strong family, a prosperous business or successful career, and a thriving church; or triumphing in life, moving in supernatural power, receiving blessings from heaven, reaching spiritual maturity, and being a man or woman of God—none of these results happens overnight or arbitrarily. Everything concerning the Spirit requires prayer, commitment, sacrifice, offerings, and death to self. We cannot expect God to do for us what He has called us to do. He has given us principles and keys, and He has revealed to us mysteries He has kept hidden from others (see, for example, Luke 10:21); it is our responsibility to do the rest.

I can give innumerable testimonies from my own life of the need for perseverance and constancy in prayer. For example, obtaining my master's degree from Oral Roberts University took me three and a half years. It required effort, persistence, and sacrifice. At the time, I already had all the burden of taking care of my family and overseeing the ministry, as well as a network of churches around the world;

but I set a goal for myself of earning my master's degree, and, with the help of the Holy Spirit, I accomplished it and graduated with honors. There are some people who want immediate success without any effort; others want breakthrough in prayer without any sacrifice. That is why the only things they receive are disappointments, doubts, and unfulfilled goals. However, because I understood the principle that breakthrough doesn't happen by chance, I now enjoy the benefits of having a diploma from one of the best universities in the United States. I know that there are many young people reading this book, and to you I say that if you are about to throw in the towel, don't do it. Persevere! If you have been battling in prayer for a miracle, don't give up. Keep going, because breakthrough is around the corner. Continue pressing on in prayer, until you see the fullness of God manifested!

3. Breakthrough Prayer Works According to the Law of Accumulation

"But when the fullness of the time had come, God sent forth His Son, born of a woman, born under the law, to redeem those who were under the law, that we might receive the adoption as sons" (Galatians 4:4–5). The phrase "fullness of time" signifies that something has been completed, has matured, or has grown until it has reached its maximum stature; it indicates the end of a time ordained by God. Remember, maturity is not reached in an instant. Just as it took centuries of preparation for the time of Christ's first coming to be fulfilled, the time of His second coming is being prepared by prayers, offerings, and sacrifices that will accumulate until the moment the Son of God is ordained to return.

The "law of accumulation" refers to the building up of something until it reaches its fullness. As mentioned earlier, God has stored up prayers that were given in the past in order to pour out the manifestations of their answers in the end times. Prayers offered by Abraham, Moses, David, the prophets, the apostles, and our beloved Jesus are stored there. The Bible says, *"Now when He [Jesus, the Lamb who was* slain] *had taken the scroll, the four living creatures and the twenty-four elders fell down before the Lamb, each having a harp, and golden bowls full of incense, which are the prayers of the saints"* (Revelation 5:8).

Have you prayed for certain things that you still haven't seen manifested? If you have offered prayers that were to be fulfilled in the future, they have accumulated in one of these heavenly bowls; as in a bank account, they are "earning interest" and growing. And they are about to be poured out! I can assure you that those prayers have not been forgotten, even though they may not manifest until the prayer bowl is full. It may be that there is not enough "spiritual matter" accumulated to give shape to your miracle in the natural realm. Therefore, continue depositing prayers, making offerings, and fasting, until the time is fulfilled and your bowl is ready to be poured out.

> There are answers to prayers that will not manifest until there is enough accumulation and the time has been fulfilled.

When you pray continuously, it is as if you generate a momentum, or impulse, that produces enough accumulation in the Spirit to be able to produce a breakthrough. (We will talk more about momentum in the next chapter.) If you are fasting and praying, and you still don't see results, you must surpass your current level of seeking God; you must build greater spiritual strength, which will accelerate the momentum to the point of breakthrough. Keep praying and don't give up until you achieve enough accumulation. The delay is over! Your time for breakthrough is now!

Breakthrough prayer involves a process comparable to the one that produces rain on the earth. Scripture says that *"if the clouds are full of rain, they empty themselves upon the earth"* (Ecclesiastes 11:3).

The law of accumulation says that, when a substance surpasses the capacity of its container, it will spill. Therefore, if you know how the law of accumulation works, you will not become discouraged that you have not yet received the answer to your prayers, because you will know that those prayers are accumulating and the manifestation of your blessing is near. Every time you pray, that accumulation grows. For example, as you continue to pray for your children's salvation, the closer they are to falling at the feet of the Lord in repentance and restoration; each time you pray for your finances, the closer you come to seeing mega-abundance. Your status is changing now! Galatians 6:9 says, *"And let us not grow weary while doing good, for in due season we shall reap if we do not lose heart."*

> The prayer of faith is "now," but breakthrough prayer requires accumulation.

Sometimes I come across people who want to see a breakthrough after giving just one offering, or after only twenty minutes of prayer. If you want to bring heaven to earth, that's not how it will happen. When your faith and prayers have sufficiently accumulated, the manifestation will take place easily.

In addition to this, you must have a specific vision of what you want to achieve. The Bible teaches us that each part of the temple in Jerusalem had specific measurements. Similarly, you need to follow the "correct measurements" in prayer. In other words, if you don't have a clear idea of what you are praying for, you will not receive the visible manifestation of what you desire—unless a sovereign act of God takes place, where human beings are not involved and accumulation is not required.

For instance, the resurrection of the dead is a powerful miracle that characterizes King Jesus Ministry. However, it was not something that happened overnight. In my daily prayers, the Holy Spirit showed me that this was the next level of power I would receive in ministry. From that moment, I started to accumulate prayers in that direction and to look for the power of the resurrection. When I had accumulated enough prayers, the bowl overflowed and resurrections began to take place. It was glorious! But it took a lot of prayer time to reach that new level.

Therefore, if you have felt the desire to stop persisting in prayer because you haven't yet seen your breakthrough, don't do it! Without realizing it, many people have allowed themselves to be overcome by discouragement, spiritual opposition, and exhaustion, and they have quit instead of carrying on until their prayers had accumulated enough to be poured out.

The Bible offers countless examples of perseverance to encourage us to keep praying. For example, after the people of Israel had entered the promised land, they arrived at Jericho, where they came across a walled city that was very difficult to penetrate. God gave specific instructions to Joshua, telling him the Israelites were to march around the city once each day, for six days, and then, on the seventh day, to march around the city seven times. After that, the people were to collectively give a loud shout while the priests blew on trumpets—and the walls would collapse. (See Joshua 6:1–5.) If Joshua had not persevered in following all the instructions God gave him, the walls wouldn't have fallen, nor would the Israelites have obtained the victory. We must do the same to obtain our breakthrough—persevere!

I know a pastor from Asia who prayed and preached for eleven years without seeing anyone receive Christ. Then, suddenly, a great revival started in his church, bringing the fruit of all those years of sowing. Today, his church has about one hundred thousand people. I could share many ministry testimonies and also accounts from history that illustrate the rewards of perseverance. One famous historical example is that of Abraham Lincoln, who ran for the U.S. Senate twice in the 1850s, without winning, but was persistent and became president of the United States of America in 1860.

> The "now" is the accumulation of faith, prophecies, prayers, fastings, offerings, and praises— ready to be poured out.

Elijah, one of the greatest prophets, faced a tremendous challenge during a time in which idolatry had become widespread in the northern kingdom of Israel. Under God's instructions, the prophet said it would not rain in Israel until he gave the word; as a result, there was a great drought in the land. (See 1 Kings 17:1.) The people turned back to the only true God after Elijah defeated the prophets of the false god Baal in a remarkable display of heavenly power. (See 1 Kings 18:20–40.) Then Elijah prayed for a breakthrough to the drought, until the clouds poured rain again:

> And Elijah went up to the top of Carmel; then he bowed down on the ground, and put his face between his knees, and said to his servant, "Go up now, look toward the sea." So he went up and looked, and said, "There is nothing." And seven times he said, "Go again." Then it came to pass the seventh time, that he said, "There is a cloud, as small as a man's hand, rising out of the sea!" So he said, "Go up, say to [King] Ahab, 'Prepare your chariot, and go down before the rain stops you.'" (1 Kings 18:42–44)

In biblical Hebrew, the number seven indicates fullness or completeness. When Elijah told his servant to go up seven times, he was really telling him to go up until the miracle was completed—until the rain-filled cloud appeared in the sky. If we don't understand this symbolism, we may become frustrated, believing that merely doing something seven numerical times will yield results for us. However, breakthrough prayer must be made "seven times" in the sense of persisting until the cloud fills with water, until the cup overflows, until the miracle manifests and we can see it with our eyes. If the fullness of time for your prayers hasn't yet arrived, you must continue to accumulate them. You must persist until you see the breakthrough.

4. Maintaining a Breakthrough Demands Perseverance in Prayer

Once we have obtained a breakthrough in any area, we must remain alert to keep from losing that breakthrough. This means that if conquering a spiritual territory required prayer, maintaining it will also require prayer. For example, some people who receive a breakthrough in their finances soon become absorbed mainly in their business and their financial transactions; they stop praying and end up forgetting about God. Sooner or later, these people will end up losing the blessing they had achieved through prayer. The same thing can happen in all other areas of life. Suppose a marriage is in crisis, and a couple earnestly prays, and God answers by bringing a breakthrough of reconciliation; however, then they stop praying, and their problems return. They have neglected to continue to protect their union. Therefore, the key to maintaining a breakthrough is to persevere in prayer and to cover with the blood of Christ that which cost us so much to achieve.

Activation

Dear reader, I encourage you to keep persisting in prayer, to continue generating momentum in the supernatural to effect a breakthrough in everything you know to be the will of God for you. Keep yourself aligned with the Word and standing in righteousness. Go back in prayer again and again until you see that the heavens open, the cup overflows, the clouds pour out the rain, and the answer to your prayer is given from the throne of God.

Before you pray, ask yourself how much you really want this breakthrough, and if you are willing to pay the price it will demand in prayers, offerings, and sacrifices. Every prayer you pray aligned with the will and timing of God will be answered, but you must persist until you see a breakthrough. Maybe you have begun to feel that God doesn't hear you or that you are wasting your time; maybe you have given up, without finding any explanation for your apparent defeat. Ask God for the grace to persevere. His grace is the supernatural power that strengthens us to persist until we see our breakthrough.

Now, allow me to say a brief prayer for you:

Beloved heavenly Father, thank You for giving us this revelation of spiritual keys to breakthrough prayer. Right now, I release Your supernatural grace upon every reader, so that they may persevere in prayer until they see their breakthrough. I declare that every spirit of delay has been defeated, and that Your power is released upon them, in order to see Your will be fulfilled on earth as it is in heaven—with healings, miracles, signs, and wonders.

Receive this breakthrough now, in the name of Jesus! And when you have received it, maintain it by surrounding it with prayer so you will never lose it.

Testimonies of Breakthrough Prayer

Raised from Her Deathbed

My name is Pastor Mirtha de Millan from Venezuela, South America, and our ministry is under the spiritual covering of Apostle Maldonado, which was crucial for me when I faced imminent death. I was born with a heart condition, and, every so often, I suffered from tachycardia [rapid heart rate]; however, a while back, that condition worsened. I started to become very fatigued and to feel tachycardia very frequently. The doctor diagnosed two accelerated valves. He prescribed some medications to control the condition, but instead of getting better, I became worse—the other two valves also became accelerated. I felt extreme exhaustion and constant tiredness, and I would often faint. At my next doctor's appointment, I was prescribed sleeping pills, but this made things even worse. By the third appointment, I was seriously ill. I couldn't stand on my own, I could barely walk, and I would often fall; I also fainted constantly. Days later, I lost all mobility; I couldn't walk or talk, and I was unable to open my eyes or move any of my limbs. I was literally bedridden. I was taken to the doctor, where I had another crisis that left me in intensive care because not enough blood was getting to my brain. Since I couldn't move, it seemed like I was asleep, but, in reality, I was conscious and desperate because I wasn't able to communicate with my family. I wanted to shout and tell them I was awake, but I couldn't.

In Venezuela, the hospitals are always crowded with people, so the doctor sent me home, monitored by two nurses. There, I suffered a stroke, and it was as if I was dead. However, my children and my husband never stopped praying for me. Among all the messages of support my family received, there was a voicemail message and prayer on the cell phone from Prophet Ana Maldonado. They put the recording close to my ear for me to hear it; my faith started to grow, and then the miracle began. In the prayer, she said, "Rise up! Walk, and get out of that circumstance!" That was a beautiful message because, three hours later, I started moving my hands. The next day, I sat up by myself in bed, without anyone's assistance. I still couldn't speak, but with my son's help, I was able to get up and start walking. I kept listening to the prophet's prayer and praying to the Lord. The next day, they took me to the doctor. When he saw me, he couldn't believe I was standing! By persevering in faith and in prayer, I was able to come through it all. My healing was complete! The doctor told me that any physical damages caused by the stroke would get better little by little, and that with time I would be able to walk normally and my twisted face would straighten out. However, I almost didn't have to wait, because my persistence in prayer led me to see the complete miracle in an accelerated way. Christ raised me up! As if that were not enough, after reviewing my new medical tests, the doctor found that I had a new thyroid gland—and I mean new, because three years earlier, I'd had it removed! God did a multiple creative miracle, in my heart and in my thyroid! I thank God and my spiritual parents for everything they have taught us about the power of prayer and about persevering until we see the complete miracle.

Breakthrough in the Acquisition of Land for a Church

I am Marta Castro, from San Antonio, Texas, United States. About a year ago, my family and I were watching one of the services from King Jesus Ministry online, and we received a strong impartation from the Holy Spirit through Apostle Guillermo Maldonado, who was talking about faith. Overcome by the presence of God, we felt we should sow one thousand dollars from our ministry into the kingdom. The financial situation of our church was not very good at that time, but we believed and sowed that sum the same day. During this period, we were looking for a piece of land on which to build a church, and we had found one for which the asking price was half a million dollars. Since we didn't have that amount, we decided to keep pushing and persevering in intercession, filling our heavenly bowl with more prayers. One day, about a year later, one of our spiritual sons went back to that property and obtained an appointment with the owner through his son. The owner said he would like to meet with the pastors. We felt the time had arrived. That day, we walked around the 9.7 acres of land, which are located on a main avenue that connects with the city center. At one point during the conversation, the owner stopped and said, "What if you buy only 3 acres for $167,989, and I sow to the church 6.7 acres?" Immediately, we knew this was a supernatural result that could only have come from the Lord. We had believed the word that was preached and had sealed it with a faith seed, trusting for a breakthrough, and the Lord gave it to us. We now have the title to a property valued at half a million dollars, purchased at only a third of its price! Next, we are going for the supernatural provision for the construction!

9

HOW MOMENTUM
ACHIEVES BREAKTHROUGH

"Pray without ceasing."
—1 Thessalonians 5:17

We have learned that in the supernatural realm, everything operates according to spiritual principles and patterns. One of these principles is that, in the kingdom, breakthrough prayer operates under the law of accumulation, which takes us *"from faith to faith"* (Romans 1:17) and *"from glory to glory"* (2 Corinthians 3:18). It is as if we are placing one brick on top of another in order to build a wall, and then continuing the same process for the next wall, until an entire house is finished.

However, when we place these "bricks" of prayer, we do not merely use a ritual repeated from memory, nor do we offer our requests in a mechanical way—what the Bible describes as *"vain repetitions"*

(Matthew 6:7). Rather, each time we pray, God gives us more revelation of His Word and purposes, and we pray fresh prayers according to what He reveals to us. We can call this pattern, which is mentioned or illustrated often in the Bible, "praying without ceasing." (See, for example, 1 Thessalonians 5:17; Psalm 88:1; Nehemiah 1:4; Acts 12:5; Romans 1:9; 2 Timothy 1:3.) In this chapter, I want to teach you how to build or create the momentum that brings breakthrough in prayer.

Through Constancy in Prayer, We Enter into Supernatural Momentum

Continuing with the above example of the construction of a house, perseverance establishes the base or foundation for the succeeding building phases. When we are constant in prayer, the Lord can work in our life because this causes us to enter into the supernatural momentum of the Holy Spirit, who brings God's plans into existence. It is clear that the more persevering we are in prayer, the closer we will be to a sudden manifestation of the supernatural. This explains why, when a person who prays continually declares something according to God's will, it happens immediately. It is supported by the momentum they have developed in their times of prayer. Remember that such results are not achieved overnight; we must first persist in faith and prayer.

As noted earlier, Jesus emphasized this reality to His disciples: *"Then He spoke a parable to them, that men always ought to pray and not lose heart"* (Luke 18:1). This verse brings to mind two important truths, which are worth reviewing here. Why should we always pray? First, prayer is necessary because, through it, we develop our relationship with the Father. Just as our body needs food in order to maintain its health and strength, our spirit and soul need prayer to maintain their health and strength. In prayer, we can receive the Father's instructions, guidance, and love, and we can be warned about coming attacks of the enemy so we can counteract those assaults. In prayer, our spiritual eyes are opened, and we can see into the supernatural realm, bind and loosen according to God's will, and win spiritual battles, leading us to manifest God's power on the earth.

Second, prayer must not be given up on. There are miracles that won't happen, situations that won't be resolved, and doors that won't open unless we persist in prayer, exerting so much pressure in the Spirit that we see a breakthrough that releases the power of God upon our lives. Again, one of the greatest problems in the church today is a lack of perseverance. So many people—men and women, adults and young people, individuals of all races and cultures—begin things but never finish them. We must finish what we have begun, and finish it well. Whenever we abandon an activity, we never realize its fullness. There are many consequences to a lack of perseverance. For example, based on my own experiences, I dare to say that many people stop fellowshipping with other believers when they abandon their prayer life. This weakens their own faith and hurts the body of Christ.

> Whoever doesn't have spiritual perseverance won't have a long-standing prayer life.

We have seen that the devil wants to interrupt the rhythm of the supernatural in us. If Satan can manage to interfere with the rhythm of your prayers, then the things you have been praying for may not manifest. Many people fail to see their miracle because the rhythm ceased right at the point that the answer was about to manifest. The enemy uses various methods to make us lose this rhythm, such as sidetracking us with the cares of life or causing us to focus on our disappointments or on the apparent delay in seeing the manifestation of our requests. The devil is ready to steal our blessings at the slightest distraction that diverts our attention. That is why developing perseverance and spiritual resistance is so important. The best way to stop the enemy is by praying without ceasing. The apostles learned this principle and made sure they taught it in all the congregations they formed. Hence, the new Christians *"continued steadfastly in the apostles' doctrine and fellowship, in the breaking of bread, and in prayers"* (Acts 2:42). Paul asked the Christians in Rome to keep themselves *"rejoicing in hope, patient in tribulation, continuing steadfastly in prayer"* (Romans 12:12).

Have you ever had the experience of praying continually over a long period of time, but then suddenly ceasing to pray, and, when you wanted to restart, you found it very difficult to do so? The reason is that you lost the spiritual rhythm of prayer. No matter how hard it might seem, I urge you to return to praying without ceasing. You can enter that rhythm again and begin to build momentum in prayer once more.

Perseverance establishes a habit,
develops a rhythm, and releases breakthrough;
but praying without ceasing sustains the blessing.

Pressure in the Spirit Breaks Matter

The simplest way I can describe perseverance in prayer is the illustration of water constantly dripping onto a rock. A small drop of water seems harmless compared to an enormous rock; however, over time, the water begins to pierce the surface of the rock until, amazingly, it penetrates it. The same thing happens in the spiritual realm. Perseverance in prayer can cause the hardest difficulty or circumstance to give way and break.

This is the pattern the first Christians applied when King Herod sent Peter to prison. *"Peter was therefore kept in prison, but constant prayer was offered to God for him by the church"* (Acts 12:5). The believers put in a claim, or demand, to heaven on Peter's behalf, based on God's will for him. Peter was about to be executed, but the demand from the church kept him alive for his apostolic purpose to be fulfilled.

> And when Herod was about to bring him out, that night Peter was sleeping, bound with two chains between two soldiers; and the guards before the door were keeping the prison. Now behold, an angel of the Lord stood by him, and a light shone in the prison; and he struck Peter on the side and raised him up, saying, "Arise quickly!" And his chains fell off his hands. Then the angel said to him, "Gird yourself and tie on your sandals"; and so he did. And he said to him, "Put on your garment and follow me." So he went out and followed him, and did not know that what was done by the angel was real, but thought he was seeing a vision. When they were past the first and the second guard posts, they came to the iron gate that leads to the city, which opened to them of its own accord; and they went out and went down one street, and immediately the angel departed from him. (Acts 12:6–10)

In modern times, many men and women of God have departed this earth and gone to be with the Lord before their time because they became sick or were in an accident, and the church didn't come into agreement to pray for them. If you know of a current case like the ones I have just described, put a demand on heaven for that man or woman of God to be preserved, for the Lord to extend His mighty arm and cause supernatural healing or deliverance to take place.

Praying without ceasing provokes a physical manifestation.

The key is to continue your momentum in prayer, because surely the breakthrough will come. The prayers for Peter were so persistent that they brought deliverance from the invisible realm to the visible realm. It didn't matter how thick the walls of the prison were, how solid the bars on his jail cell were, how strong the chains holding him were, or how many guards were watching him, because when the church prayed, the supernatural ruled over the natural. Prayer takes us into a realm where chains can be broken, walls can be walked through, and buildings—and lives—can be shaken, such as happened to the believers after an earlier release of Peter and John from prison. About this, the Scripture says that *"when they had prayed, the place where they were assembled together was shaken; and they were all filled with the Holy Spirit"* (Acts 4:31).

It is clear that, in the realm of prayer, natural laws can be put on hold and spiritual laws can take over. The third chapter of the book of Daniel tells us the story of three Hebrew young men who had a lifestyle of prayer to the one true God and were thrown into a fiery furnace for refusing to worship the golden image King Nebuchadnezzar had erected—or any of his other gods. Here again, the supernatural surpassed the natural, because although the executioners raised the temperature of the blazing furnace, the young men didn't burn up. Instead, they freely walked around in the fire. The king's astonishment and alarm at the sight was such that he said to his counselors, *"Did we not cast three men bound into the midst of the fire?... I see four men loose, walking in the midst of the fire; and they are not hurt, and the form of the fourth is like the Son of God"* (Daniel 3:24–25).

Moreover, the prophet Daniel, who *"knelt down on his knees three times [a] day, and prayed and gave thanks before his God"* (Daniel 6:10), saw firsthand how the physical world bowed to the spiritual when he was later thrown into a den full of hungry lions for worshipping his God. Although he was left with the lions the entire night, God preserved his life.

When [King Darius] *came to the den, he cried out with a lamenting voice..., "Daniel, servant of the living God, has your God, whom you serve continually, been able to deliver you from the lions?" Then Daniel said to the king, "...My God sent His angel and shut the lions' mouths, so that they have not hurt me, because I was found innocent before Him; and also, O king, I have done no wrong before you." Now the king was exceedingly glad for him, and commanded that they should take Daniel up out of the den. So Daniel was taken up out of the den, and no injury whatever was found on him, because he believed in his God.*

(Daniel 6:20–23)

If we want to change the state of sickness, poverty, depression, or curses in which people live, we must create enough momentum in the Spirit through prayer that we reach the point where the laws of the physical world and the norms of human experience are no longer significant. I declare that right now, as you read this book, chains of addiction, depression, cancer, and poverty in your family are broken. Every curse upon you or your house is destroyed now, in the name of Jesus!

> In the realm of prayer, natural laws can be put on hold and spiritual laws can take over.

Perseverance Creates Momentum in the Spiritual Realm

In the natural world, momentum is the force, power, or propulsion that an object gains while it is in motion. During momentum, there is a point at which an object reaches its maximum impulse. When a long jump athlete reaches his full momentum, he gives his best jump. Similarly, in the spiritual realm, when we continue to pray, we reach the precise measure of accumulated prayers that brings the spiritual atmosphere into its fullness, producing a supernatural impulse that brings the breakthrough.

Jesus knew that to produce miracles, He had to build spiritual momentum. That is why *"He Himself often withdrew into the wilderness and prayed.... And the power of the Lord was present to heal them"* (Luke 5:16–17). Jesus operated in the spirit of increase, which always seeks more from God—accumulation, growth, and expansion. Today, we must pray more and with greater revelation than we did yesterday, until we reach the necessary peak of momentum. Many people don't receive answers to their prayers because they are trapped in the past, praying the same things all the time; yet, as we have noted, believers— whether as individuals or corporately—should always pray something fresh, putting something new into the spiritual atmosphere. This adds to the momentum, until it reaches its fullness.

Persistent and continuous prayer maintains supernatural activity in a church.

If you have persevered in prayer, not losing heart, you now have enough spiritual momentum to declare what you want to happen. Your prayers have generated the power to bring change. At King Jesus Ministry, we have intercessors praying twenty-four hours a day, and when one prayer shift ends, the person in the next shift who continues in prayer must be in the same spirit as the previous intercessor and enter with the same momentum that has already been built, in order to keep building the spiritual atmosphere. It is like a relay race in which the first runner is completing his lap, and the next runner has to match his speed in order to receive the baton smoothly and with unbroken stride. If you are praying in a group for something in particular, don't stop praying until another person enters into prayer with the same momentum you have. Then you will see miracles, because the atmosphere will become full, creating the spiritual impulse for a breakthrough.

> The church must generate enough momentum in prayer to give birth to the new things God wants to do. If nothing new happens, it's because there is no spiritual momentum.

We create spiritual momentum with our praises, worship, prayers, offerings, and declarations of faith—everything accumulates in the Spirit and pushes the breakthrough. When you stop building the atmosphere, the momentum stops. That is why we must keep the atmosphere growing until it is brought to its fullness. Acts of faith also contribute to momentum. For example, when someone preaches about miracles but doesn't seek to demonstrate what they're proclaiming by leading the people who are in need to take a corresponding action of faith, the momentum stops. This means that when we move from words to actions, we are also building momentum.

A positive response of faith from a group of people is another factor that generates momentum in the manifestation of miracles. The opposite happened to Jesus when He entered His hometown of Nazareth, where there was very little faith and where He was not well-received. "*Now He could do no mighty work there, except that He laid His hands on a few sick people and healed them*" (Mark 6:5). The spiritual atmosphere in Jesus's hometown was so dry that it couldn't conduct the power that He carried. Jesus came empowered by prayer, ready to do miracles, but He encountered an apathetic people who rejected His ministry—and forfeited the answers to their needs.

Momentum Produces Breakthrough

It is in the context of the second coming of Christ that the Bible instructs us to *"pray without ceasing"* (1 Thessalonians 5:17). Jesus is coming for a church that prays, and that does so continually. Everything begins with consistency, persistence, and perseverance, which produce momentum—and momentum is what brings breakthrough. When breakthrough occurs, yokes are broken and chains fall off; everywhere, people are healed and delivered, and miracles are manifested. As the accumulated prayers produce breakthrough in the now, walls of opposition are dismantled, limitations are removed, and strongholds are knocked down.

So again, if you have accumulated prayers, prophecies, offerings, and fastings; if you have sown into the kingdom and given to those in need; if you know the promises contained in God's Word and have treasured them in your heart—then the clouds are full and ready to pour out their reserves of blessings, miracles, and wonders. Remember, *"if the clouds are full of rain, they empty themselves upon the earth"* (Ecclesiastes 11:3). Yes, if you have done all these things, it is impossible for breakthrough *not* to take place. Your blessing is about to be poured out. These are the times of breakthrough! There will not be any more delay!

Activation

Beloved reader, all the tools to achieve a breakthrough have been placed in your hands. You only have to persevere in prayer until the gates of heaven are opened upon your life, until every attack from the enemy ceases, until your children return home, until your marriage is restored, until your ministry is activated, until the prophecies upon your life and your ministry are fulfilled, until you find your husband or wife, until your womb becomes fruitful, until your business produces profits and prosperity is released, until each and every one of God's plans for your life—and for all the earth—is fulfilled.

Testimonies of Breakthrough Prayer

Allow me to share some personal testimonies of answered prayer, so that you will better understand how to achieve a breakthrough. About twenty-five years ago, I met an elderly woman whose calling was breakthrough intercession. She explained to me how this kind of prayer worked. For example, God would suddenly lead her to intercede for a person or a situation; something in her spirit would mobilize her, and without knowing exactly what it was about, she would start praying continually. Sometimes, she would pray for one or two hours; other times, she would keep praying for days, weeks, even months—until she felt the breakthrough. One day, she asked God, "Why do You place burdens on me to pray for so many different people?" His answer was, "Because I don't have other people who pray the way you do. There are some to whom I give the burden, but they don't pray until they get a breakthrough." On one occasion, God moved her to pray for one man in particular. She prayed until she felt the breakthrough. A week later, she found out that the man had been in a terrible accident with a truck and that no one could explain how he had survived. Then she understood why she'd had to pray for him so much.

In my case, from the moment I converted to Christ, I understood that without prayer, I could not have a relationship with God or change the negative circumstances or impossible situations I faced in my life. I knew that only through prayer could I govern over the physical realm and have victories in the Spirit. As a new Christian, I still didn't know how to pray very well, but I would seek God with passion. One day, I started feeling a great spiritual burden for the salvation of my family. At that time, I had been a believer for only for a few months, and I was the only one in my family who was a Christian. But the burden for my family moved me to pray, and I spent three days fasting and praying without ceasing! Without knowing what I was doing, I started praying in tongues, with perseverance, for the salvation of my family.

After the first day had gone by, everything in the situation remained the same; then the second day went by, with no news of salvation. Only by the third day was I able to achieve a spiritual momentum. I felt that something was breaking and the change was beginning. That spiritual perseverance had produced a momentum and led me to experience a breakthrough. Then, I felt an uncontainable joy—so much so, that I couldn't stop laughing. I heard the voice of God telling me, "Your family is in My hands." Within six months, my whole family had received Christ.

One of the signs that a breakthrough has taken place is that abundant peace, joy, and laughter will come upon you.

Throughout my ministry, I have been able to achieve a great number of breakthroughs through prayer, on both a personal and ministerial level. For example, when my wife and I started pastoring the church in Miami, many people told us that the city was under a curse. African, Haitian, and Cuban witches had made occult pacts and decreed that Miami was "the pastors' cemetery." Consequently, when a church's congregation exceeded two thousand people, the pastor either died, got cancer, or fell into sin, and then the church would close. It didn't matter if the church was Anglo-Saxon, Hispanic, or African-American—it would fall. Around that time, our church was reaching that number, but we were not willing to let ourselves be defeated.

One night, we held a prayer vigil from eight in the evening until three in the morning, which the entire leadership attended. We exerted so much pressure in the Spirit, and the atmosphere was charged in such a way, that, suddenly, we heard a sound such as a race car makes when it accelerates. It was an acceleration in the Spirit that all of us could hear and feel. Then God told me, "The curse upon the city has been broken!" Starting that day, the growth of our church skyrocketed. Throughout the years, we have multiplied that number more than five times. But that's not all. Today, Miami has several churches with more than five thousand members, due to that breakthrough we achieved in the Spirit. The atmosphere in the city changed, and the curse was broken, as a result of perseverant prayer. Because of the pressure we exerted in the Spirit, we now enjoy spiritual freedom and the growth of the gospel in the city of Miami.

However, such breakthroughs are not happening only on a local level, because my calling has always included bringing the supernatural power of God to all the nations of the earth. Before I was a pastor, I traveled to almost every country in Latin America as an evangelist, preaching the message of Jesus. Once we established the ministry in Miami, God told me He would open the African continent to me. After that, I started praying without ceasing in that direction. Some doors opened, but I felt that it was not God who had opened them; it was as if the atmosphere wasn't the right one in which to go. So, I kept praying. One day, someone invited me to a television network to manifest the power of God, and there the breakthrough started! God used that door to give me access to Africa. After many years of prayer, by His grace, we have now been doing crusades on that continent for more than ten years, gathering more than a million people to hear the Word of God each time.

In the past two years, we have also gained access to Ethiopia, thanks to Apostle Tamrac, my spiritual son there. In those crusades, we have seen more than a million people receive Christ into their hearts! We have been able to record hundreds of testimonies of the manifestation of the power of God, although we know that there are many more. We have seen multitudes set free from demonic attacks, receive miracles and healings, and be activated in the supernatural power of God. Now, other nations are hungry to see the move of the Spirit. Our TV program is broadcast throughout the African continent, and millions are being touched and transformed by God. Once more, this is the result of our having persevered in prayer until the African continent opened for us to go there and preach the gospel of the kingdom.

Another breakthrough was our entrance into the Asian continent. God had told me He would open a portal in Asia for me to take His gospel. As soon as I received that word, we started praying without ceasing until we saw it happen. Right now, we are on television in China, and we have gone to Taiwan, Malaysia, and Hong Kong, filling stadiums and holding conferences for thousands of people to be saved and transformed. Malaysia is a country with a population that is 80 percent Muslim, but perseverant prayer produced the spiritual breakthrough that allowed us to preach about the true God there, for the salvation of many. At the final meetings in Malaysia, more than forty thousand people gathered in a stadium for two nights. One evening, the power of God raised twenty-one disabled people from their wheelchairs, without anyone but the Holy Spirit touching them! The meetings in

Hong Kong were also powerful, with eight thousand people in attendance. These breakthroughs in Asia have occurred due to my prayers and the prayers of my wife, my team of pastors, and my spiritual children around the world, as well as the faithfulness of all others who, with perseverance, pray and intercede for us.

Dear reader, it is possible to achieve breakthroughs of this kind not only in the United States, Africa, or Asia, but in any country and continent in which you may live. It is possible to achieve breakthroughs in your marriage, your family, your church, your business, your education, and in any other area of your life.

We must not grow weary and give up. If we persevere, push, and create momentum, even when we don't see anything happening, and if we keep praying in tongues, giving offerings, and doing righteous acts, every day and at all times, we will see the greatest revival we have witnessed in our lives—in our cities and in our nations, to the ends of the earth. The key is to persevere in prayer, to have a holy stubbornness that prevents us from stopping before we create the momentum that will bring the breakthrough—a momentum that will surpass natural limitations and push us beyond what is hindering us. It is possible!

I could provide additional testimonies of breakthrough about businessmen and women who received provision and favor, about couples whose marriages were strengthened and healed, about families that were restored, and about children who not only were released from the grip of the world and returned home, but were also radically transformed by the power of God. In all these instances, perseverance caused hindrances and opposition in the physical and spiritual realms to yield, and activated change in the minds and hearts of people. Such breakthroughs are also available for you, beloved reader!

I pray that the Lord will give you the grace and favor not to give up or cease interceding. I pray that losses, discouragement, persecution, and criticism won't make you abandon prayer but that, on the contrary, they will push you to pray until you see breakthrough and receive all that God has promised you. *Do not give up!* Persevere until you achieve a breakthrough!

WATCHING AND PRAYING FOR CHRIST'S RETURN

"Watch therefore, and pray always that you may be counted worthy to escape all these things that will come to pass, and to stand before the Son of Man."
—Luke 21:36

The night before His crucifixion, Jesus went to the garden of Gethsemane to pray, as was His regular practice. (See Matthew 26:36; Luke 22:39.) Gethsemane, located on the Mount of Olives, means "oil press" and refers to a place where olives were crushed in a mill to extract their oil. It was also the place where Jesus was pressed to the maximum, tempted to abandon His purpose—where His anguish was so great that He even sweat drops of blood. Yet it was also the place where He surrendered His will to do the will of the Father. Even though His physical death took place at Golgotha, it was at Gethsemane that Jesus defeated death, because, knowing in the Spirit all He would have to suffer, He made the firm decision to voluntarily surrender His life to redeem humanity from sin.

Jesus certainly knew what He was going to face on the cross the next day, and that is why He told His disciples, *"Sit here while I go and pray over there.' And He took with Him Peter and the two sons of Zebedee, and He began to be sorrowful and deeply distressed"* (Matthew 26:36–37). The full humanity of Jesus is evident in the emotions He manifested and in His desire to have His three closest disciples by His side to support Him in this time of crisis. But they didn't understand their Master's request and fell asleep.

> Christ's command was to "*watch and pray.*"

Let's look at the whole picture of the situation in which Jesus told His disciples to watch and pray. His ministry on earth was almost at an end; Jesus knew He didn't have much time left and that He would be betrayed, because the Father had revealed it to Him in prayer. He took three of His disciples and asked them to watch with Him while He prayed. The account continues:

> *He went a little farther and fell on His face, and prayed, saying, "O My Father, if it is possible, let this cup pass from Me; neverthe-less, not as I will, but as You will." Then He came to the disciples and found them sleeping, and said to Peter, "What! Could you not watch with Me one hour? **Watch and pray**, lest you enter into temptation. The spirit indeed is willing, but the flesh is weak." Again, a second time, He went away and prayed, saying, "O My Father, if this cup cannot pass away from Me unless I drink it, Your will be done." And He came and found them asleep again, for their eyes were heavy.* (Matthew 26:39–43)

The command Jesus gave to His disciples to *"watch and pray"* (similar to His earlier commands in Mark 13:33 and Luke 21:36 about watching and praying for His return) was the same directive that, many years later, the apostles Paul and Peter gave to the early church. (See Ephesians 6:18; 1 Peter 4:7.) It is also the command that the disciples of Christ must follow now, in the end times. Watch and pray!

> When God gives a command,
> it is because there is no other option.

What Does It Mean to Watch and Pray?

Jesus asked His disciples to watch and pray so they wouldn't be tempted to move outside the Father's will. The word *"watch"* implies being spiritually awake. It indicates paying close attention, being very cautious, being ready, prepared, and alert. It means to discern, perceive, and be in the Spirit. To be able to see in the spiritual realm is a gift of the outpouring of the Holy Spirit. This ability is very important in prayer, especially in the end times.

Watching is the complement of praying because each is a condition of the other. It is not possible to really pray without being alert, and it is not possible to watch without the support of prayer. When we watch, nothing takes us by surprise, because our spiritual senses are vigilant. We are like a radio whose dial is set in the correct position to receive the signal transmitted from a broadcast station. If we stay tuned to heaven, we will always know how to pray and how to act.

When we watch, we are also like sentries posted in high towers, where they have a commanding view of their surroundings, enabling them to spot the approach of enemy invaders so their city can defend itself in time. The country of Israel is in a permanent state of alert due to constant attacks from its enemies. For this reason, its surveillance is one of the most sophisticated in the world, with the most up-to-date radar capabilities and highly trained sentinels. If they didn't have that surveillance system, their territory might be bombarded until it was completely devastated. Spiritually, we need to be in that kind of constant alertness and readiness.

> An army without surveillance capability is operating blind, because it cannot anticipate an attack.

In the Old Testament, the prophet Habakkuk understood the purpose of the "prayer tower," which is why he said, *"I will stand my watch and set myself on the rampart, and watch to see what He will say to me"* (Habakkuk 2:1). If a church doesn't have such a prayer tower, it cannot intercept the enemy's plans to attack it. This is why I believe one of the assignments of the prophets of our time is to be watchmen on the wall. *"I have set watchmen on your walls, O Jerusalem; they shall never hold their peace day or night. You who make mention of the* LORD, *do not keep silent"* (Isaiah 62:6). As the watchmen in the church, through prayer, prophets receive strategies for spiritual battle, because they can see the activity of the enemy and know how to counteract it.

> Prophetic prayer is about praying from what is perceived and seen in the Spirit.

Watching also implies anticipating or expecting. We watch for God to work because we have the confidence that we will see manifested what we are declaring in prayer. Once more, let us note the importance of being expectant when we pray. If we don't antic-ipate any answers, then why do we make requests? It might actu-ally happen that the Lord answers your prayer but you don't see His answer because, when you lost your expectation, you stopped watching for its manifestation. This is why we need to be able to perceive and see in the Spirit. The more you watch, the more spir-itually sensitive you will become, and the more conscious you will be of what is happening around you in the spiritual realm. Your spiritual sight will become clear.

> As we pray from what we perceive and see in the Spirit, we must remain watchful for what we will receive from God.

Jesus didn't say "pray and watch," but *watch and pray*," in that order, because if we watch, we will be in a good position to pray effectively and powerfully. Moreover, our prayers will cease to be monotonous, composed of empty words that come from our minds but don't proceed from our hearts or carry the revelation of the Spirit. Why do some people feel that prayer is boring? Because their prayers are full of "vain repetitions," without enthusiasm or expec-tation. Vain repetitions are "filler prayers" consisting of phrases that are easy to say and keep us in our comfort zone. You urgently need to get out of that zone and start praying what you see spiritually. For example, today, start telling God something you have never told Him before; speak to Him as a Father, and you will immediately note the difference.

> Spiritual perception is the ability to see inward and forward.

Remember that God wants you to pray according to what you perceive. To watch and pray is to declare the mind of God. As you pray, you start seeing more and, in consequence, you continue declaring and decreeing according to what you see. Frequently, the Lord speaks to us through dreams and visions, and we as the church are responsible for watching and praying to interpret them correctly.

Watching—or Sleeping?

Jesus has given the church this command to "watch and pray," and there is no alternative! After our Lord finished praying in the garden of Gethsemane, we see that *"He came and found them* [His disciples] *asleep again, for their eyes were heavy"* (Matthew 26:43). From God's perspective, when we don't watch, we are spiritually asleep. My question is, if what you're asking God for is so important, why do you "fall asleep" while praying about it?

What does it mean to be asleep in the Spirit? It means to be insensitive to what is happening around us. Even worse, it is to be cold or indifferent before the presence of God; it is to break the bond of communion with Him, showing an apathy toward, or a lack of interest in, the things of the Spirit—resulting in disconnection, separation, and distance from Him.

Our assignment during prayer is to be a watchman for our family, our church, and the things of God. A thief will never enter a house if he knows he's being watched. In the same way, if Satan and his demons are planning to attack you, but they see that you are vigilant and aware of their plot, they will not be able to carry out their invasion; or you will perceive when they are trying to invade, and you will be able to stop them or activate the alarms. One way or another, the enemy will realize that access is blocked, and he will have to flee. But if you are like the disciples whom Jesus took to Gethsemane to watch with Him—who, instead of praying, fell asleep—you will leave the access open and won't offer any resistance to the enemy.

We can conclude that because the disciples weren't able to watch, but drifted into sleep, they fell into temptation when Jesus was arrested and crucified. With sadness, I must admit that this is the condition of the church of Christ today. It is asleep, insensitive to the times in which we are living, to the movements of the Spirit, to the needs of people—and to how the enemy is working against it. As a result, Christians are prone to fall into temptation. After having traveled through many countries preaching the Word of God and seeing the condition of the church, my conclusion is that the body of Christ is not prepared for His second coming.

> If we are not watching and praying, we are not ready for Jesus's return.

In the gospel of Luke, Jesus talked about His second coming, saying, *"But take heed to yourselves, lest your hearts be weighed down with carousing, drunkenness, and cares of this life, and that Day come on you unexpectedly"* (Luke 21:34). Here Jesus lists some of the things that cause us to be spiritually asleep, the opposite of having an alert and vigilant spirit. The enemy seeks to invade the territories of our health, marriage, children, finances, and vocation, but we don't realize it because we aren't watching. The church doesn't perceive satanic attacks against it because it is asleep. How can we say that we are ready to receive Christ in His second coming if we are spending most of our time solving problems that have come upon us because we have not watched and prayed?

> The devil can attack your life only when you don't watch, because what you anticipate, you can prevent.

The Parable of the Wise and Foolish Virgins

In the parable of the ten virgins in Matthew 25, the five foolish virgins had the same kind of lamps that the five wise virgins had. This means that, at some point, they were also wise. Spiritually speaking, they once had a relationship with God and their lamps were filled with the oil of the Spirit. But they stopped watching, and without their realizing it or caring, the oil was consumed, and they didn't go back to get resupplied. They ended up disconnected and insensitive to the move of God. They fell asleep! In the same way, the church today has generally lost its communion with God; it is spiritually asleep and doesn't have any expectations that He will move. The anointing "ran out" because the Holy Spirit has been disregarded, or He has not been given enough room to move with freedom and power in the congregations. The worst part is that neither the leaders nor the people notice this lack, since they don't have a vital relationship with the Spirit. Meanwhile, the church continues to sleep and be unprepared for the second coming of Jesus.

> The biggest consequence of being spiritually asleep will be not perceiving the second coming of Christ.

Purposes of Watching and Praying

Consequently, there are two fundamental reasons why it is essential that we learn to watch and pray in a growing and continuous way.

1. To See the Second Coming of the Lord

In the twenty-first chapter of Luke, Jesus announced the signs of the end of the age and of His return. In verse 36, He warned, "*Watch therefore, and pray always that you may be counted worthy to escape all these things that will come to pass, and to stand before the Son of Man.*" The second coming of Christ is related to the prayer life of His church. For this reason, God is in the process of restoring the church's prayer life and demanding that Christians learn to watch. Do you think Jesus can come for a church that is asleep? Do you think He can return for a church that is insensitive to His presence, that doesn't have oil in its lamp, that lacks the anointing and power of the Holy Spirit? Do you think Jesus can come for a church that doesn't have a relationship with Him? No! Jesus is coming for a glorious bride, without *"spot or wrinkle"* (Ephesians 5:27), one that remains alert and is ready to manifest His power.

> The Lord will come for those who watch and pray; the survival of the church depends on it.

It is obvious that not watching or praying can bring serious consequences to the church. The direst consequence is that, because the church in general has restricted the movements of the Holy Spirit and has become insensitive to the presence of God, it is deaf to the voice of God and blind to the strategies of the enemy. Having wonderful preachers, building beautiful church buildings, producing professional television programs, and organizing vast social outreach projects are all good things, but they will not help the church escape the terrible events of the end times. The only way the trials and *"great tribulation"* (Matthew 24:21) coming on the earth will not reach us is if we are always watching and praying.

> God will not destroy the righteous with the unrighteous.

Essentially, most of the church doesn't really believe in the second coming of the Lord. How do we know this? Because the believers are not watching or praying; therefore, they are not anticipating His return. If they believed in His coming, they would be watching and praying without ceasing, as the Scripture tells us to do. If you do not watch, it's because you don't have an expectation of something happening. It is when we are vigilant and prayerful that the Spirit reveals to us that Christ is coming soon.

We are so blessed to be the generation that will see the second coming of Christ! All the signs have been fulfilled. He is about to come; therefore, we must understand the importance of watching and praying, since only by these means will we be ready to be "caught up to meet Him in the air" at His return. (See 1 Thessalonians 4:17.)

> We must watch and pray until Christ returns.

Thanks to God, there is a remnant of believers who are watching and praying, who always live in expectation of His return. If you are asleep, you cannot stay that way! You must be ready for His return and prepared to go with Him.

2. To Prevent Entering into Any Temptation from the Enemy

Don't forget that what we can see in advance, we can prevent. The enemy will be able to attack us only when we are off guard. Temptation usually comes in the times of our greatest weakness, and if we aren't watching, we will yield to it. That is why Jesus said to His disciples, *"Watch and pray, lest you enter into temptation. The spirit indeed is willing, but the flesh is weak"* (Matthew 26:41).

When we stop watching, we become insensitive to the Spirit, we compromise truth, we sin against God, and the enemy defeats us.

When the disciples whom Jesus had asked to watch with Him finally woke up, the enemy was already in the place, and the soldiers and officers of the chief priests and Pharisees were approaching the Master to apprehend Him. Everything happened so suddenly for the disciples that it took them by surprise; they didn't know what to do because they hadn't seen what Jesus had seen in prayer. They had limited themselves to only reacting to the situation, because they weren't prepared for it. Consequently, Peter attacked a servant with his sword, but Jesus told Peter that His time had come, and He healed the servant's ear. (See, for example, John 18:3–11; Luke 22:47–51.) It was all confusion and desolation for the disciples, because they had not been alert and praying.

The devil knows when we are not prepared, because we simply react. In contrast, those who watch don't merely react; nothing takes them by surprise, because they are awake and prepared. They know what God is doing and also what the enemy is doing, and they know the next step they're going to take. Thus, the only time the devil can come close to our life is when he sees we are unprotected because we are not watching. When we are vigilant, he discreetly moves back.

Temptation and sin always come when we don't watch.

No temptation has overtaken you except such as is common to man; but God is faithful, who will not allow you to be tempted

beyond what you are able, but with the temptation will also make
the way of escape, that you may be able to bear it.
(1 Corinthians 10:13)

As we watch and pray, God will show us how to face or flee any temptation, and how to solve every problem. The disciples fell into temptation because they didn't watch and pray. Because Jesus watched and prayed, when He was tempted to abandon His purpose—knowing in prayer everything that would happen to Him—He surrendered His will and chose to give His life to save humanity.

> Being vigilant allows you to close every entrance to the enemy.

Jesus taught that we must ask the Father, *"Do not lead us into temptation"* (Matthew 6:13). However, we must comprehend that temptation enters our life when we are not watching. That is why, through prayer, when we see temptation coming, we can counteract it before something bad happens. Some intercessors who have not been well-trained accept everything they see in the Spirit as being inevitable—even the attacks of the enemy—instead of praying without ceasing until they're able to destroy the works of the devil and achieve a breakthrough.

The reason God shows us the plans of the enemy is to give us the opportunity to destroy them or avoid them. When we pray in the Spirit, we see what is about to happen, but that doesn't mean it has already happened in the natural dimension. We are perceiving what the enemy is trying to do; it is the devil's activity in the spiritual sphere—although he doesn't know that God is showing it to us. That is the advantage we have if we watch. We can prevent it from coming to pass.

> "Do not lead us into temptation" also means
> "Let me not surrender or give in to temptation."

The Bible teaches us that *"each one is tempted when he is drawn away by his own desires and enticed. Then, when desire has conceived, it gives birth to sin; and sin, when it is full-grown, brings forth death"* (James 1:14–15). This means that our will is involved in the process of temptation. If we see the plan that the enemy is plotting against us, we can prepare beforehand, by an act of our will, to stand strong in obedience and stay in a place of righteousness. We can pray that God will strengthen us to remain in Him. In this way, we can cut off the cycle of sin before it begins. Therefore, when the enemy tempts us, we must resist, or, if necessary, flee from the temptation. We only fall into the trap of temptation when we don't watch to anticipate the plans of the devil, because it is usually only the blind or the careless person who stumbles over visible obstacles. If the church watches and prays, it won't fall into temptation or the snares of the enemy.

Guidelines for Watching and Praying

You may be asking yourself, *Well, how do I watch and pray? How do I apply all this knowledge to my life?* Below are some guidelines to help you put into practice what you have learned up to this point.

1. Continually Pray in the Spirit

As Christians, it's important that we know how to strengthen our spirit in the faith, as the Bible teaches us to do in Jude 1:20: *"But you, beloved, building yourselves up on your most holy faith, praying in the Holy Spirit."* Of course, you cannot build up your spirit if it is asleep! It must first awaken and get up! If you pray in the Spirit, you will be able to see in the spiritual realm, but if you neglect to do this, your vision will be limited. Every time I pray in the Spirit, I am alert to what God is telling me and to what He is doing; that way, I can align myself with His plans for the now. As children of God, we must be in tune with the momentum the Holy Spirit is bringing, because it is the momentum of the now.

2. Constantly Be Filled with the Spirit

Our spirit needs to be filled with the Spirit of God. Can Jesus come for a bride who is not filled with His Spirit? Will He come for a bride who is not anointed? Of course not. Jesus commanded the church to live in a state of fullness in the Spirit. The person who is not filled with the Holy Spirit lives in a limited dimension. The Spirit cannot work in us unless we maintain a certain level of prayer. Similarly, a sinner cannot be transformed in an environment of nominal or religious Christianity. In these days, we must live continually filled with the Holy Spirit, having our lamps full of oil for the vigil.

> Our spirit should continually call to and attract God's Spirit.

Before we conclude, I must reemphasize this point: We need to watch and pray in the Spirit because the return of the Lord is near! We must be alert and prepared for His coming. It is essential that we see and perceive what is happening around us in the spiritual realm. This is not a time to sleep! The enemy diligently works against us—especially when he sees that we're not watching. If watching and praying will help to prevent us from succumbing to future temptations and attacks, then we can't stop watching and praying! We must pray without ceasing in the Spirit, being alert to perceive what God is saying and doing, and we must always be ready for what is to come. This should be our lifestyle.

Activation

You are reading this book because Jesus is calling you—just as He did His disciples—to watch and pray with Him, without ceasing. I encourage you to answer that call and start giving priority to your relationship with God in prayer, being in expectation of what He wants to show you in spiritual intimacy. Look ahead in the Spirit to what is coming for your family, for your ministry, for your city, and for the world. Be sensitive to the presence of God, to His will, and to the needs of other people; additionally, be alert to what the devil is plotting to do or is already doing. You can anticipate and defeat the enemy!

Prepare also for the second coming of Christ, maintaining a lamp filled with the oil of the Spirit. Be like the good watchman who doesn't fall asleep but is vigilant in his duties. Be vigilant to maintain the blessings of God, to protect your family, to surround your ministry with angels, and to keep the doors open for the gospel to be preached and the supernatural to be manifested in your nation and every nation of the world. Watch so that you will not be tempted to abandon the purpose of God for your life; watch in order not to be snared by the traps of the enemy, who wants to lead you into sin and cause you to fall far from the grace of God. Stand on the will of God, on His Word, and on His righteousness, so you may see all your prayers answered. And finally, generate the necessary spiritual momentum for the answers to your prayers to be manifested instantly.

Throughout this book, I have taught you how to pray in order to obtain a breakthrough. Now, do it yourself! Be constantly filled with the Spirit of God and prepare to receive the King of Kings as a member of that pure bride, without spot or wrinkle, who watches for the return of her Groom, Jesus Christ. He promised it—and He will fulfill it! Watch and pray! Christ is coming soon!

SELECTED BREAKTHROUGH PRAYERS IN SCRIPTURE

Moses's Intercession for the Israelites to Prevent Their Destruction

*And the L*ORD *said to Moses, "Go, get down! For your people whom you brought out of the land of Egypt have corrupted themselves. They have turned aside quickly out of the way which I commanded them. They have made themselves a molded calf, and worshiped it and sacrificed to it, and said, 'This is your god, O Israel, that brought you out of the land of Egypt!'" And the L*ORD *said to Moses, "I have seen this people, and indeed it is a stiff-necked people! Now therefore, let Me alone, that My wrath may burn hot against them and I may consume them. And I will make of you a great nation." Then Moses pleaded with the L*ORD *his God, and said: "L*ORD*, why does Your wrath burn hot against Your people whom You have brought out of the land of Egypt with great power and with a mighty hand? Why should the Egyptians speak, and say, 'He brought them out to harm them, to kill them*

*in the mountains, and to consume them from the face of the earth'?
Turn from Your fierce wrath, and relent from this harm to Your
people. Remember Abraham, Isaac, and Israel, Your servants, to
whom You swore by Your own self, and said to them, 'I will multiply your descendants as the stars of heaven; and all this land that I
have spoken of I give to your descendants, and they shall inherit it
forever.'" So the* Lord *relented from the harm which He said He
would do to His people.*   (Exodus 32:7–14)

Daniel's Intercession for the Israelites to Be Forgiven and Restored to Their Land

In the first year of Darius the son of Ahasuerus, of the lineage of the Medes, who was made king over the realm of the Chaldeans— in the first year of his reign I, Daniel, understood by the books the number of the years specified by the word of the LORD through Jeremiah the prophet, that He would accomplish seventy years in the desolations of Jerusalem. Then I set my face toward the Lord God to make request by prayer and supplications, with fasting, sackcloth, and ashes. And I prayed to the LORD my God, and made confession, and said, "O Lord, great and awesome God, who keeps His covenant and mercy with those who love Him, and with those who keep His commandments, we have sinned and committed iniquity, we have done wickedly and rebelled, even by departing from Your precepts and Your judgments. Neither have we heeded Your servants the prophets, who spoke in Your name to our kings and our princes, to our fathers and all the people of the land. O Lord, righteousness belongs to You, but to us shame of face, as it is this day—to the men of Judah, to the inhabitants of Jerusalem and all Israel, those near and those far off in all the countries to which You have driven them, because of the unfaithfulness which they have committed against You. O Lord, to us belongs shame of face, to our kings, our princes, and our fathers, because we have sinned against You. To the Lord our God belong mercy and forgiveness, though we have rebelled against Him. We have not obeyed the voice of the LORD our God, to walk in His laws, which He set before us by His servants the prophets. Yes, all Israel has transgressed Your law, and has departed so as not to obey Your voice; therefore the curse and the oath written in the Law of Moses the servant of God have been poured out on us, because we have sinned against Him. And He has confirmed His words, which He spoke against us and against our judges who judged us, by bringing upon us a great disaster; for under the whole heaven such has never been done as what has been done to Jerusalem. As it is written in the Law of Moses, all this disaster has come upon us; yet we have not made our prayer before the Lord our God, that we might turn from our iniquities and understand Your truth. Therefore the Lord has kept the disaster in mind, and brought it upon us; for the Lord our God is righteous in all the works which He does, though we have not obeyed His voice. And now, O Lord our God, who brought Your people out of the land of Egypt with a mighty hand, and made Yourself a name, as it is this day—we have sinned, we have done wickedly! O Lord, according to all Your righteousness, I pray, let Your anger and Your fury be turned away from Your city Jerusalem, Your holy mountain; because for our sins, and for the iniquities of our fathers, Jerusalem and Your people are a reproach to all those around us. Now therefore, our God, hear the prayer of Your servant, and his supplications, and for the Lord's sake cause Your face to shine on Your sanctuary, which is desolate. O my God, incline Your ear and hear; open Your eyes and see our desolations, and the city which is called by Your name; for we do not present our supplications before You because of our righteous deeds, but because of Your great mercies. O Lord, hear! O Lord, forgive! O Lord, listen and act! Do not delay for Your own sake, my God, for Your city and Your people are called by Your name." Now while I was speaking, praying, and confessing my sin and the sin of my people Israel, and presenting my supplication before the Lord my God for the holy mountain of my God, yes, while I was speaking in prayer, the man Gabriel, whom I had seen in the vision at the beginning, being caused to fly swiftly, reached me about the time of the evening offering. And he informed me, and talked with me, and said, "O Daniel, I have now come forth to give you skill to understand. At the beginning of your supplications the command

went out, and I have come to tell you, for you are greatly beloved;
therefore consider the matter, and understand the vision."

(Daniel 9:1–23)

The Disciples' Prayer for Power to Preach the Gospel

And [Peter and John] *being let go* [after being taken into custody for preaching the resurrection of Jesus], *they went to their own companions and reported all that the chief priests and elders had said to them* [having being ordered not to teach in the name of Jesus]. *So when they heard that, they raised their voice to God with one accord and said: "Lord, You are God, who made heaven and earth and the sea, and all that is in them, who by the mouth of Your servant David have said: 'Why did the nations rage, and the people plot vain things? The kings of the earth took their stand, and the rulers were gathered together against the* LORD *and against His Christ.' For truly against Your holy Servant Jesus, whom You anointed, both Herod and Pontius Pilate, with the Gentiles and the people of Israel, were gathered together to do whatever Your hand and Your purpose determined before to be done. Now, Lord, look on their threats, and grant to Your servants that with all boldness they may speak Your word, by stretching out Your hand to heal, and that signs and wonders may be done through the name of Your holy Servant Jesus." And when they had prayed, the place where they were assembled together was shaken; and they were all filled with the Holy Spirit, and they spoke the word of God with boldness.... And with great power the apostles gave witness to the resurrection of the Lord Jesus.* (Acts 4:23–31, 33)

_____

_____

_____

_____

_____

Paul's Prayer for the Ephesians to Receive Spiritual Wisdom and Revelation

Therefore I also, after I heard of your faith in the Lord Jesus and your love for all the saints, do not cease to give thanks for you, making mention of you in my prayers: that the God of our Lord Jesus Christ, the Father of glory, may give to you the spirit of wisdom and revelation in the knowledge of Him, the eyes of your understanding being enlightened; that you may know what is the hope of His calling, what are the riches of the glory of His inheritance in the saints, and what is the exceeding greatness of His power toward us who believe, according to the working of His mighty power which He worked in Christ when He raised Him from the dead and seated Him at His right hand in the heavenly places, far above all principality and power and might and domin-ion, and every name that is named, not only in this age but also in that which is to come. And He put all things under His feet, and gave Him to be head over all things to the church, which is His body, the fullness of Him who fills all in all.

(Ephesians 1:15–23)

EXCERPTS FROM
BREAKTHROUGH FAST

Fasting is an integral part of prayer and has its own significant spiritual principles and patterns. Since I wasn't able to cover all these critical points in *Breakthrough Prayer*, I have written a whole book on the topic, entitled *Breakthrough Fast: Accessing the Power of God*. I pray that you will be blessed and strengthened by the following excerpts from that book:

Introduction: The Power of Fasting

We are living in the prophetic *"times of restoration of all things"*:

*Repent therefore and be converted, that your sins may be blotted out, so that times of refreshing may come from the presence of the Lord, and that He may send Jesus Christ, who was preached to you before, whom heaven must receive **until the times of restoration of all things**, which God has spoken by the mouth of all His holy prophets since the world began.* (Acts 3:19–21)

The word *restoration* means "a bringing back to a former position or condition." It indicates being returned to original intent. In these last days, God wants to restore the church's intimate relationship with Him and empowerment in His Spirit so we can complete His purposes—spreading the gospel of the kingdom throughout the world, bringing salvation, healing, and deliverance. This restoration includes a stirring in the church to return to living by the Spirit—no longer relying on our own strength and techniques for serving God—and to prepare for the second coming of Jesus Christ.

The book of the prophet Joel describes the end-time restoration of all things, which involves both Israel and the church. In chapters 1 and 2, the prophet describes the desolation of Israel and calls for repentance and fasting. But in chapter 2, we read this word from the Lord about restoration: *"I will restore to you the years that the swarming locust has eaten, the crawling locust, the consuming locust, and the chewing locust, my great army which I sent among you"* (Joel 2:25). The third and final chapter of Joel deals with God judging the nations and blessing His people.

What is our responsibility in God's plans for restoration? The promises of God require our personal cooperation by prayer and fasting. Fasting is an essential tool for being empowered by the Spirit; it will enable us to experience breakthroughs in the spiritual realm, especially as we incorporate it as an integral part of our lifestyle. As I wrote in my book *Breakthrough Prayer*, "with a breakthrough, what we need is brought from the spiritual world to the natural world, so that we can see it in a visible or tangible demonstration of God's power or provision." This principle of the necessity of prayer and fasting applies not only to restoration on a global scale but also to restoration in our individual lives, right now, by God's power and provision—in our personal life, marriage, family, finances, ministry, and anything else that needs to be healed, repaired, or given new life.

> ## The "times of restoration of all things" include a return to prayer and fasting.

Fasting Is a Spiritual Sacrifice

Since ancient times, fasting has been a spiritual sacrifice offered to God by His people. We see fasting practiced in both the Old and New Testaments. Sometimes, God ordained or urged a particular fast for His people; other times, individuals, groups, or nations initiated a fast due to a need. One Old Testament example of God calling for a fast is the following: *"'Now, therefore,' says the LORD, 'turn to Me with all your heart, with fasting, with weeping, and with mourning'"* (Joel 2:12). Previous to this word, the prophet Joel had proclaimed: *"Declare a holy fast; call a sacred assembly. Summon the elders and all who live in the land to the house of the LORD your God, and cry out to the LORD"* (Joel 1:14).

In another example, the prophet Daniel initiated a fast for the restoration of the Israelites to their land:

> *In the first year of Darius the son of Ahasuerus, of the lineage of the Medes, who was made king over the realm of the Chaldeans—in the first year of his reign I, Daniel, understood by the books the number of the years specified by the word of the LORD through Jeremiah the prophet, that He would accomplish seventy years in the desolations of Jerusalem. Then I set my face toward the LORD God to make request by prayer and supplications, with fasting, sackcloth, and ashes.* (Daniel 9:1–3)

In the New Testament, we note that Jesus fasted, and we can clearly see how vital fasting was in His life. Jesus didn't confront and overcome the great temptations by Satan in the desert until, being filled with the Spirit, He engaged in a lengthy fast—after which He began His ministry empowered by the Holy Spirit.

> *Then Jesus, being filled with the Holy Spirit, returned from the Jordan* [after His baptism] *and was led by the Spirit into the wilderness, being tempted for forty days by the devil. And in those days He ate nothing, and afterward, when they had ended, He was hungry.... Now when the devil had ended every temptation, he departed from Him until an opportune time. Then Jesus returned in the power of the Spirit to Galilee, and news of Him went out through all the surrounding region.*
> (Luke 4:1–2, 13–14; see also Matthew 4:1–11; Mark 1:12–13)

Jesus was the purest and holiest Person to walk the face of the earth. He had no sin, yet, as a human being, He still needed to pray and fast in order to defeat the enemy, know the Father's will, and firmly establish His ministry on earth. How much more do we need to pray and fast! We have been wonderfully redeemed by Christ and given the gift of the Holy Spirit. Even so, we still battle against the sinful nature, which continually tries to reassert authority over our lives (see, for example, Romans 7:22–25), and, sadly, we have a tendency to drift away from a close relationship with God. Additionally, we require ongoing power for ministry. As we fast and pray in God's presence, He provides us with wisdom, strength, and anointing.

There are additional examples of fasting in the New Testament. Jesus gave His disciples instructions about fasting, and we will look at those teachings in coming chapters. (See Matthew 6:16–18; 17:14–21.) Moreover, the biblical record shows that the believers in the early church practiced fasting as an important part of their lifestyle. For example, the prophets and teachers of the church in Antioch prayed and fasted, after which they received a word from the Holy Spirit about the ministry of Paul and Barnabas. (See Acts 13:1–3.)

Furthermore, we read in 2 Corinthians that Paul fasted often. (See 6:4–5; 11:27.) Paul wrote about half of the books in the New Testament, and he was probably the greatest apostle of all time—and yet he felt the need to regularly fast. The most powerful men and women of God have followed a lifestyle of prayer and fasting.

> **Fasting was vital to the life and ministry of Jesus. The same holds true for His followers today.**

Praying and Fasting as a Lifestyle

However, even with the emphasis on fasting in the Bible and the examples of the power of fasting in the lives of believers from early times up to the present, the body of Christ today has largely disregarded fasting! This is one reason why there is a lack of power in the church as a whole—with few miracles, signs, healings, deliverances, and other manifestations of the supernatural. Why has fasting essentially been abandoned by God's people? There are various reasons, such as overscheduled lives and even laziness, but perhaps one of the most significant reasons has been the prevalence of a "hyper-grace" outlook. This perspective says that since Christ has redeemed us and conquered the enemy, there is nothing we need to contribute to our spiritual growth and safeguarding. It is true that we can freely receive all the benefits Christ won for us on the cross. However, we must appropriate His provision by faith and apply it to all aspects of our lives. And we have a responsibility as God's priests to offer Him spiritual sacrifices of prayer and fasting in order to further His purposes in the world—and in our own lives. Thus, we must return to God's original intent for the church—becoming a people who can demonstrate His love, power, and glory while defeating the works of the enemy. The only way we can do this is to return to both prayer and fasting as a lifestyle. I can testify to the power of fasting; so many breakthroughs that I have seen in my personal life, ministry, and finances have come through prayer and fasting.

If today's believers only knew the spiritual power in fasting, they would practice it more! Many people do not understand what fasting means to God, what it can accomplish in their lives, and how it can enable them to defeat the schemes and attacks of the enemy. At this time in human history, we are living in the midst of upheaval and revolution—both in the natural world and in the spiritual sphere. As the second coming of the Lord draws near, we are dealing with demonic powers that have never before been seen on the earth. Our need to pray and fast has intensified, because only by these means can we be prepared to confront and overcome the destructive forces of the enemy.

Breakthrough Fast will help you discover this path that gives access to the power of God. It provides life-changing revelation from the Word of God and many personal testimonies about the power of fasting. You will learn what, exactly, fasting is; different types of fasts and their benefits; how to fast effectively; how to obtain and increase spiritual power through fasting; and specific guidelines and steps to making fasting part of your lifestyle. The value of fasting is incalculable—in your own life and for the future of the world. Make it part of your lifestyle starting today. Jesus said, "*Your Father who sees* [your fasting] *in secret will reward you openly*" (Matthew 6:18).

What Does Fasting Accomplish?

Fasting yields many rewards—spiritual, mental, and physical. In this chapter, we will focus on twelve spiritual benefits of fasting. These areas are interrelated, but each is a distinct benefit.

1. Keeps Our Spiritual "Edge" Sharp

If you want your spirit to become alert, then begin to fast. The more spiritually attuned you are, the quicker you will be able to perceive realities in the supernatural realm. When you fast, God begins to sharpen your ability to see, hear, and discern those realities. Fasting helps us not only to gain but also to maintain our "edge" in the Spirit, readying us to be used for God's purposes. Many believers have lost their spiritual edge, with the result that they are now functioning more in the natural realm than the spiritual domain. Whenever we lose our edge, our spiritual perceptiveness and authority are weakened, and we start to function like a nominal believer or even like someone who does not believe in God and His power.

2. Purifies Our Soul

When you fast, you also help to keep your soul (mind, will, and emotions) under the control of your spirit—taking all errant, disobedient thoughts captive to the obedience of Christ. (See 2 Corinthians 10:5.) Our spirit interacts and has connections with our soul—the moral seat of our life. By exposure to the atmosphere and influences of the world (the mind-set hostile or indifferent to God), our soul accumulates spiritual impurities and contaminations, mixtures of truth and error, and so forth. Thus, God has to strip our souls of these elements. (See, for example, James 4:8.) In fasting, we surrender all this to God. He sets us apart for Himself once again and cleanses us anew through His Word (see Ephesians 5:25–27) and Spirit.

Accordingly, during a fast, God won't usually reveal Himself to us until He first shows us the state of our inner being and the direction in which our life has been going. He will reveal where we have strayed from His truths and purposes. After we fast, our souls should be cleansed, bringing us into deeper fellowship with the Father and better equipped to serve Him.

> During the first part of a fast, God always detoxes and cleanses our souls.

3. Accelerates Our Death to "Self"

John the Baptist said of Jesus, *"He must increase, but I must decrease"* (John 3:30). As believers, we should want to lift up Jesus by our lives so that many people will come to know Him and receive His salvation and deliverance. In line with the cleansing of our souls, fasting is one of the quickest ways in which we can die to "self"— our willfulness or desire to do things our own way rather than God's way. God has wonderful plans for us, but we hinder them because we think we know better than He does. As we fast, God begins to confront us with various issues that need to be resolved. At the time, we may feel He is taking away some things that are important to us or have defined our lives. However, the more He deals with and removes these issues, the more He gives of Himself and His blessings. In this process, fasting places our lives under submission to the lordship of Christ. The priorities of the world fade away, and heaven comes into greater focus for us.

We all have something we need to give up to God—either negative elements we must let go of to be all that we were created and redeemed to be, or personal preferences that are interfering with our relationship with Him. It might be a bad temper, envy, discord, spiteful thoughts, unforgiveness, or sexual immorality. Or it might even be an unhealthy relationship, a superfluous activity, or a certain goal we've been pursuing. We can't allow any person, activity, or pursuit to become an idol in our life. To experience true life, we need more of God and less of us. When we fast, we make a decision to give up what is holding us back from God in order to receive more of Him. Fasting accelerates this death to "self."

> Fasting changes you, not God. When fasting is part of your lifestyle, you will live in a place of continual death to self—and life in God.

4. Crucifies Our Flesh

"Those who live according to the flesh set their minds on the things of the flesh, but those who live according to the Spirit, the things of the Spirit" (Romans 8:5). The *"flesh"* is also referred to as the "old man," the carnal nature, the sinful nature, or the Adamic nature. Fasting breaks down the power of the flesh very quickly in our lives. That is one reason why the enemy hates it when we fast. He wants us to remain spiritually weak and ineffective.

The Scriptures say, *"Those who are Christ's have crucified the flesh with its passions and desires"* (Galatians 5:24). Before we start fasting, the flesh, rather than our spirit, is more in control of our lives. This explains why fasting is difficult for us in the beginning. We have to break out of the natural realm and the operations of the flesh. We must live differently from the way we normally do by denying ourselves the pleasure of certain food. Then God begins to change us. He sets us apart for Himself once again. *"So I say, walk by the Spirit, and you will not gratify the desires of the flesh"* (Galatians 5:16).

Fasting is God's weapon for dealing with the flesh.

When you are living according to the flesh, you can't perceive spiritual things. *"The natural man does not receive the things of the Spirit of God, for they are foolishness to him; nor can he know them, because they are spiritually discerned"* (1 Corinthians 2:14). However, when we fast, the Holy Spirit becomes a greater reality to us than anything in the natural world. With a heightened perception of the spiritual realm, we also become more aware of the enemy and his schemes, and how to deal with them. This enables us to be prepared for whatever difficulties may come our way.

When a personal crisis looms, which is more real to you—the presence of the Spirit or the problem? When sickness comes upon you, or you receive a negative report from the doctor, which is more real to you—the power of the Spirit or the illness? When a financial emergency arises, which is more real to you—prosperity in the Spirit or lack? When fasting puts your flesh under subjection to the Spirit, heaven becomes more real to you than the temporal situations of earth.

Your fasting communicates to your flesh, in effect, "Shut up! I won't listen to you. You don't dictate to me—you are not my master; you are my servant." When the Spirit begins to take control, you become more spiritual than natural, and this is reflected in your thoughts, words, and actions.

Until the Holy Spirit becomes your greater reality, the flesh will dominate your life.

5. Breaks Our Negative Thought Patterns and Cycles

As we have seen from the above points, the beginning of a fast does the work of capturing our attention so we will allow God to remove the negative ways of thinking and behaving we have fallen into, including destructive patterns that need to be broken. We can become stuck in undesirable mental and emotional cycles, continually repeating the same negative thinking and mistakes without understanding how we became trapped in them. When we fast, God sets us free from these patterns and cycles and releases us into new cycles of life. Some negative patterns of thinking and behaving include discouragement, depression, fear, panic attacks, sadness, thoughts of death, sexual immorality, addiction, and so forth. These must be broken through fasting and prayer. If you are suffering from any of these hindrances, initiate a fast to break free from them and remove them from your life now. Reach out to another believer or group of believers who can pray, fast, and stand with you until you receive deliverance.

> The purpose of fasting is to set you free,
> not to harm you.

6. Stirs Up Our Anointing

Therefore I remind you to stir up the gift of God which is in you through the laying on of my hands. For God has not given us a spirit of fear, but of power and of love and of a sound mind.
(2 Timothy 1:6–7)

Is it possible to have the anointing and the gifts of the Holy Spirit but not have spiritual activity in your life? Yes, it is possible. This happens when the gifts and the anointing are dormant, or asleep. If this is the case, they need to be activated.

When we allow our gifts or anointing to fall dormant, we will go through a season of dryness and emptiness. By neglecting or rejecting what the Holy Spirit has given us, and not allowing Him to work in our lives, we can grieve or quench Him. The Greek verb for *"stir up"* in the above verse means to "re-enkindle." Another way of looking at it is a reawakening or arousing from sleep. Dormant areas of our spiritual life need to be awakened again. Additionally, there may be areas of giftedness in your spirit that have never before come to the surface, which the Holy Spirit wants to activate in you. You may not even know they are there. In both of these situations, we can stir up or awaken our anointing by prayer and fasting. When we fast, the gifts within us will begin to be stirred up, or activated, including gifts of the Spirit and ministry gifts. (See, for example, 1 Corinthians 12; Ephesians 4:11–12.)

People who are not inclined toward fasting miss out on manifestations of God's anointing and ways in which God desires to spread His kingdom in the world. When I want to increase the anointing in my life, I proclaim a fast and follow it, and the effects are immediate. Miracles and healings occur more quickly. Deliverances are vastly more powerful. These results are a sign that the anointing has increased. All believers need to cultivate the anointing in their lives through fasting. Start waking up spiritual activity in your life now!

> Fasting is an important way to cultivate the anointing in our lives.

7. Sharpens Our Spiritual Perception

As noted earlier, fasting is a means by which our souls are purified, so that we are able to see and hear more clearly in the spirit realm. It becomes easier for us to discern the voice of God and to learn the directions and instructions He has for us. When we are controlled by the flesh, we are blocked from discerning and perceiving in the Spirit. Fasting purifies and brings clarity to our spiritual vision. The spiritual realm begins to come into focus for us.

Fasting and prayer accelerates spiritual perception because we are enabled to see beyond the world's reality of people, events, and circumstances. We become less sensitive to the natural dimension and more sensitive to the spiritual domain and its reality. There have been times when I have sought God for something, but I was unable to receive it, even when I prayed a lot. But then, when I engaged in a fast, I heard His voice and received the answer. Why couldn't I hear God beforehand? It was because my soul had not been cleansed, and my spirit had not been sharpened. Fasting prepared me to discern and receive the answer I needed.

> Fasting causes our spiritual perception to become clear and precise. The more spiritual we become, the quicker we perceive the spiritual realm.

8. Draws Us Closer to God

To have true life, we must be in communion and union with our heavenly Father. The Spirit reveals more of the Father to us as we pray and fast in the name of His Son Jesus—enabling us to know Him better and draw closer to Him in intimate relationship. One practical reason for this result is that when we set aside time for fasting, we spend more time in prayer in God's presence. This allows us to grow in our knowledge of His character and ways.

Fasting brings us closer to God because it is a spiritual sacrifice that He honors.

9. Establishes Discipline in Us

Fasting trains us to discipline ourselves, putting our body under submission to our spirit. We place constraints on our appetite and desire for food, and in so doing, we develop self-control. Fasting strengthens us to say no to the cravings of the flesh and the temptations of the enemy. Paul wrote, *"I discipline my body and bring it into subjection, lest, when I have preached to others, I myself should become disqualified"* (1 Corinthians 9:27).

People who practice fasting develop strong discipline.

10. Causes Spiritual Breakthrough

There are certain negative forces at work in the spirit realm that will not yield until you pray and fast. You might be experiencing a crisis in your family, finances, health, or work. The enemy has constructed a wall to contain you because you have been giving to God and serving Him. Now is the time to press through to breakthrough by prayer and fasting. That trial, tribulation, or circumstance will not shift until you fast and pray.

One time, Jesus rebuked a demon from a boy after His disciples had been unable to cast it out. When they asked Him why they had not been successful in bringing deliverance, Jesus said:

> *Because of your unbelief; for assuredly, I say to you, if you have faith as a mustard seed, you will say to this mountain, "Move from*

*here to there," and it will move; and nothing will be impossible for you. **However, this kind does not go out except by prayer and fasting.*** (Matthew 17:20–21; see also Mark 9:29)

Jesus said *"this kind"*—a specific demonic entity—couldn't be removed without prayer and fasting. We need to take note of His statement in our day. Because we are in the end times, Satan has released many powerful evil spirits on the earth. Among those entities are spirits of antichrist, sexual immorality, rebellion, lawlessness, witchcraft, occultism, false religion, oppression, secular humanism, religiosity, intellectualism, and more. These spirits know they don't have much time left before their judgment by God, so they are out tracking the earth, seeking to harm and destroy. They are blocking millions of believers, putting limitations and barriers on them, and hindering their advancement in the kingdom. They have created crises, overwhelming circumstances, and mountainous problems in the lives of many Christians, who desperately need a breakthrough. Remember, a breakthrough is a sudden spiritual burst that pushes you beyond your limitations and into deliverance and freedom. Unless we pray and fast, we cannot win the victory over such attacks, achieving breakthrough.

> High-ranking, demonic spirits are not defeated without prayer and fasting.

There was an incident in the ministry of Paul in which he was confronted by an evil spirit in a slave girl, but he did not immediately cast out that spirit. He waited days before doing so. I believe he may have been fasting during that time for spiritual power to defeat the demon.

Now it happened, as we went to prayer, that a certain slave girl possessed with a spirit of divination met us, who brought her masters much profit by fortune-telling. This girl followed Paul and us, and cried out, saying, "These men are the servants of the Most High God, who proclaim to us the way of salvation." And this she did for many days. But Paul, greatly annoyed, turned and said to the spirit, "I command you in the name of Jesus Christ to come out of her." And he came out that very hour. (Acts 16:16–18)

Do you need a breakthrough now? Is something blocking you from moving forward? Is anything limiting or constraining you? Are you facing danger? Is your body sick? Are you in the middle of spiritual warfare? Are you facing a crisis in your mind or emotions? Do you need a miracle? I believe this is the time for you to proclaim a fast. Your spirit needs to be stretched and expanded to a higher capacity in order to birth extreme and unusual victory in the spirit realm. Demons perceive when we are walking in a higher dimension of power and authority, and fasting is one of the ways we appropriate that power and authority. Thus, after you complete the fast, and the breakthrough takes place, you will gain credibility in the spiritual realm, just as Paul did.

11. Sustains the Flow of the Supernatural

As I noted earlier, whenever I become aware of reduced spiritual activity in my life, I go back to fasting and praying, and I immediately see an increase in the anointing. Almost everyone who has walked in the supernatural and had a miracle ministry has had a lifestyle of fasting and praying, which sustains a continuous flow of the supernatural.

This generation of believers wants a shortcut to the power of God.

12. Is a Means of Appropriating Power

In all of the above points, we see that fasting is a means of appropriating the power of God for wisdom, healing, deliverance, the anointing, miracles, and much more. Over and over again, I have had the experience of completing a fast and seeing an increase of spiritual power and authority in my life. I have seen miracles and deliverances occur more quickly, as well as massive healings, greater faith, and other spiritual activity. When you fast, a law of exchange takes place. Fasting is a sacrifice of yourself. You give of yourself to God, and, in return, He gives you supernatural power. He makes deposits of heavenly power into your life as you pray and fast.

ABOUT THE AUTHOR

Apostle Guillermo Maldonado is the senior pastor and founder of King Jesus International Ministry (Ministerio Internacional El Rey Jesús), in Miami, Florida, a multicultural church considered to be one of the fastest growing in the United States. King Jesus Ministry, whose foundation is built upon the Word of God, prayer, and worship, currently has a membership of nearly seventeen thousand. The ministry also offers spiritual covering to a growing network of over three hundred churches that extends throughout the United States and globally in Latin America, Europe, Africa, Asia, and New Zealand, representing over six hundred thousand people. The building of kingdom leaders and the visible manifestations of God's supernatural power distinguish the ministry as the number of its members constantly multiplies.

Apostle Maldonado has authored over fifty books and manuals, many of which have been translated into other languages. His previous books with Whitaker House are *Divine Encounter with the Holy Spirit*, *How to Walk in the Supernatural Power of God*, *The Glory of God*, *The Kingdom of Power*, *Supernatural Transformation*, and *Supernatural Deliverance*, all of which are available in both English and Spanish. In addition, he preaches the message of Jesus Christ and His redemptive power on his national and international television program, *The Supernatural Now* (*Lo Sobrenatural Ahora*), which airs on TBN, Daystar, the Church Channel, and fifty other networks, with a potential outreach and impact to more than two billion people around the world.

Apostle Maldonado has a doctorate in Christian counseling from Vision International University and a master's degree in practical theology from Oral Roberts University. He resides in Miami, Florida, with his wife and ministry partner, Ana, and their two sons, Bryan and Ronald.